JAMS
PICKLES &
CHUTNEYS

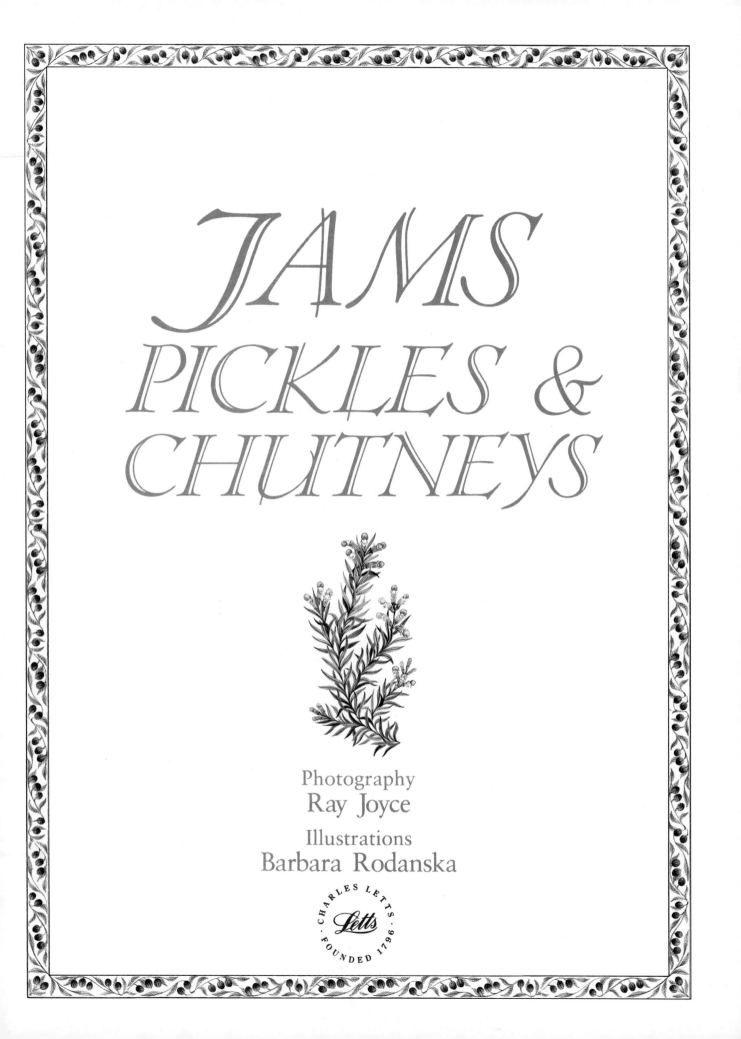

Photography
Ray Joyce

Illustrations
Barbara Rodanska

CHARLES LETTS
Letts
FOUNDED 1796

THE PUBLISHER THANKS
THE FOLLOWING FOR
THEIR ASSISTANCE IN THE
PHOTOGRAPHY FOR THIS
BOOK:

AVALON BICYCLE CENTRE

BEACH ROAD
RESTAURANT

CAMELLIA GROVE
NURSERY

PEACH AND LAVISH
FLORISTS

ROYAL DOULTON

SIRIUS

TEE JAYS ANTIQUES

VILLAGE LIVING

VILLEROY AND BOCH

WARDLAW PTY LTD

WATERFORD WEDGWOOD

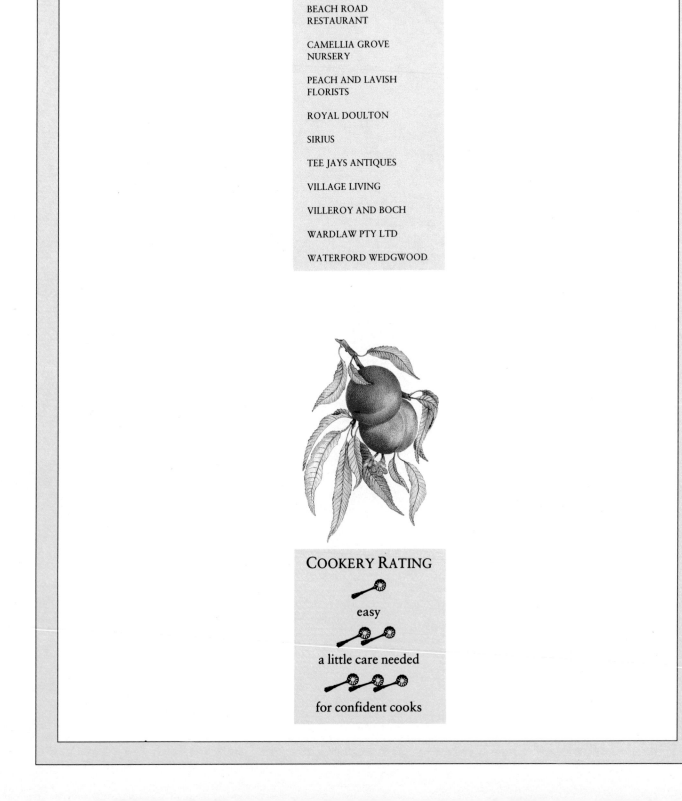

COOKERY RATING

easy

a little care needed

for confident cooks

CONTENTS

JAMS, PICKLES and CHUTNEYS

INTRODUCTION

Preserving in the home has made a revival in the eighties and will continue well into the nineties. People are enjoying the fruits of their labour and realising the result is well worth the time and effort involved. This has been reduced considerably since our grandmothers' day, when everything had to be done by hand. With labour saving devices in our kitchens and fast clean cooking appliances available, the pleasurable aspect of this old-fashioned skill has greatly increased.

EQUIPMENT

Like all tasks, it is far easier and more successful if the correct utensils are used. A few good basic pieces of equipment and utensils are essential.

Large Saucepan or Preserving Pan A pan with a heavy base is essential in obtaining even cooking with no scorching or burning on the base. Aluminium, stainless steel and enamel pans are suitable to use. However, avoid using enamel pans that are chipped; enamel pans often develop 'hot spots' which encourage preserves to catch on the base. Copper and iron pots are not suitable to use when preserving. The pan should be large enough to enable the mixture to boil rapidly without boiling over and wide enough to allow the mixture to evaporate quickly, which in turn shortens the cooking time. (The pan should be only half full when all the ingredients are added.) Use saucepans with short looped handles that are securely attached; a long handle often cannot support the weight of the mixture and becomes dangerous when carrying hot jams and chutneys.

KITCHEN UTENSILS

Spoons Spoons should be long handled to avoid burns from hot mixtures. Metal spoons are required for skimming the surface of jams and chutneys and wooden spoons are required for stirring hot mixtures. Ensure wooden spoons have not picked up flavours from other uses that may taint the preserve.

Wooden Boards Necessary to place hot pots on after cooking. If wood is unavailable, laminex, cork or other heatproof material is suitable. Due to the extremely high temperatures that preserves reach during cooking it is important the pot is not placed on a kitchen surface that will be permanently damaged. Boards are also necessary for the cutting and chopping of the ingredients. Choose wood or plastic boards in preference to boards with a hard surface; this assists in keeping knives sharp.

Measuring Equipment Kitchen scales, measuring spoons and jugs are essential in taking the guesswork out of the correct proportion of ingredients. Accurate measuring is the key to success.

Large Bowls Essential to preserving, particularly when ingredients need to stand overnight. Glass, earthenware and stainless steel are suitable for this. Avoid using plastic which has a tendency to pick up strong flavours. A copper bowl may discolour the food unless it has a stainless steel lining.

Sugar Thermometer A thermometer is an asset when checking the setting point of jams and jellies. If a thermometer is unavailable, there are other reliable methods whereby the setting point can be tested; these will be discussed later in the book.

Jam Funnels These assist when filling jars with hot mixtures. Preserves may be poured from a heatproof jug which is quite successful in obtaining a clean fill.

Jars Purchasing new jars to store preserves in is certainly the easiest way, though it is not always practical and often an expensive exercise. If you are using jars that have been used before it is well worth the effort involved in preparing them. Remove the labels by soaking in hot water and detergent until the bulk can be lifted off. The remainder can be removed using acetone or nail polish remover. Jars that have had a strong-flavoured food stored in them will often still retain the odour of the food. It is essential to clean the jars thoroughly before using them for bottling preserves.

Sometimes the smell seems to persist, but you will find that it is the lid, not the jar, that is to blame. Often soaking in water and vanilla and then drying in the sun can prove successful. If odours cannot be removed completely, then avoid bottling preserves with delicate flavours using these lids. Choose jars that have plastic or plastic coated metal lids. It is important that metal lids are kept out of contact with vinegar mixtures which will corrode the metal, giving a metallic flavour to the preserve. If jars are without lids, jam covers or melted wax may be used to seal the jars. Jam covers are available at supermarkets, some newsagents and health food shops.

Food Processor While not necessary, it certainly reduces the time spent in chopping, slicing and grating. A sharp knife is a *must*; without one it is difficult to obtain an even result and using a blunt knife increases the time spent in cutting.

Cheesecloth Handy to tie spices in during cooking, making it easy to remove at the end of cooking.

POINTERS FOR PERFECTION

Ingredients
• Choose good quality fruit and vegetables. Fruit should be slightly under-ripe and vegetables should be at their peak. Old vegetables have woody texture which will affect the resulting product.
• Choose good quality vinegars to use in chutneys, pickles and relishes. Lesser quality vinegars often are not acidic enough to be effective in preserving. The flavour of quality vinegars is far superior and worth the extra money.
• Unless the recipe states otherwise the sugar used when preserving is generally white crystal sugar. This gives a clear result to jams and jellies. Brown sugar, molasses, treacle, honey and golden syrup are sometimes called for; however this is normally as a flavouring rather than a preservative, so it is often combined with white sugar. Sugar substitutes are unsuitable to use in jams and jellies that rely on sugar as the preserving agent.

Sterilising Jars
• Jars must be sterilised to prevent the growth of micro-organisms. After ensuring jars are thoroughly cleaned with labels removed, rinse in very hot water and place upside down on a rack to drain.
• Warm jars in a slow oven (150°C) and use jars straight from oven; this prevents the jars from cracking when being filled with the hot mixture.
• Lids should be boiled or rinsed in very hot water and allowed to drain.

Sealing
• Ensure preserves are sealed correctly. A good seal is essential in keeping the preserve in optimum condition. Preserves may be sealed with just the lid of the jar, providing it has a plastic or plastic coated metal lid. A metal lid is suitable to use on jams provided a double piece of waxed paper is placed between the lid and the surface of the jam.
• Melted wax may be poured onto the surface of the cold preserve. If using this method of sealing it is advisable to set a piece of string into the surface of the wax; this makes it easy to remove the wax. Ensure the preserve is filled above the neck of the bottle, otherwise the wax sets below the neck forming a seal wider than the neck of the bottle and difficult to remove.
• Jam covers may be used; these are clear pieces of cellophane-like material. Prior to using, the seals are dipped in vinegar or water, placed over the jars containing the hot preserve and sealed with a band. On cooling, the seals shrink giving an airtight seal to the preserve. These seals work well with jams; however they should be used only for short term storage of pickles, chutneys and relishes since the vinegar mixture will begin to evaporate and this will affect the keeping quality of the preserve.
• Wipe around rim of bottles with a damp cloth prior to sealing. This ensures the edge of the rim is clean, giving a good seal.

Labelling and Storing
• Label and date preserves at the time of making, including a use-by-date. When further quantities are made, rotate stock to use the older preserve first.
• Store preserves for at least a few days to mellow flavours. (In the case of chutneys a few weeks is better.)

Summer

Summer's gift of fresh stone fruits includes peach, plum, apricot, nectarine and cherry, all flavour-filled, with juicy flesh and vividly coloured skins. Use them at their peak to produce deliciously sweet jams and jellies and refreshingly sharp and spicy pickles and chutneys. Indulge family and friends with Melon and Peach Conserve or try Apricot Butter, Spiced Peaches and traditional Bread and Butter Cucumbers.

Nectarine Jam spread as filling in a basic cream sponge

SUMMER JAMS

Melon and Peach Conserve
11

Orange Watermelon Jam
11

Nectarine Jam
12

Black Cherry Jam
12

Peach and Ginger Jam
12

Peach and Passionfruit Jam
15

Honeydew and Pineapple Jam
15

Tomato Jam
15

Apricot Butter
17

Blueberry and Apple Jelly
17

Tropical Nut Jam
18

Plum Jam
18

Apricot Conserve
18

Melon and Peach Conserve

Combine equal quantities of Melon and Peach Conserve and orange juice. Add 2 tablespoons peach liqueur, heat and pour over waffles and ice-cream.

PREPARATION TIME: *40 minutes plus overnight standing.*
COOKING TIME: *1 hour*
MAKES *1.25 litres*

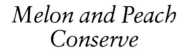

1 large rockmelon (5 cups, diced)
7 large peaches (5 cups, diced)
3 oranges
¾ cup orange juice
5 cups sugar
½ cup lemon juice

1   Peel and finely chop the rockmelon. Peel, stone and dice the peaches. Peel and finely chop oranges. Place rockmelon, peaches and oranges in a large bowl. Pour over orange juice and sugar. Leave to stand overnight.

2   Transfer to a large saucepan or boiler and cook uncovered for 30 minutes until conserve begins to thicken. Stir in lemon juice and continue cooking another 20–30 minutes or until thick.

3   Remove from heat and stand 3 minutes. Poor into warm, sterilised jars and seal. When cool, label and date.

Orange Watermelon Jam

Combine 600 mL plain yoghurt with 200 mL Orange Watermelon Jam. Dissolve 2 tablespoons of gelatine in ¼ cup orange juice. Heat in microwave to dissolve. Add to combined yoghurt mixture with 2 tablespoons grated orange rind. Allow to partially set. Whip 300 mL thickened cream and fold through. Spoon into glass serving dishes. Chill to set. Serve with chilled watermelon slices and orange segments.

PREPARATION TIME: *40 minutes plus 2–3 hours standing*
COOKING TIME: *1¾ hours*
MAKES *1.25 litres*

1 large ripe watermelon (remove rind and seeds)
4 cups sugar
1.5 kg oranges
1 cup water

1   Slice watermelon into slivers and measure to make about 1 kg pulp. Place in a large bowl with 2 cups of sugar and let stand 2–3 hours. Peel and seed enough oranges to make 1 kg. Slice oranges thinly and set aside. Remove white pith from 2 of the orange peelings; cut the rind into thin strips and reserve.

2   Put watermelon mixture into a heavy based saucepan or boiler. Heat to boiling, then simmer, stirring frequently, 50 minutes. Meanwhile in another large heavy saucepan, dissolve remaining 2 cups of sugar in water. Add sliced oranges and reserved strips of rind. Heat to boiling, reduce heat and simmer, stirring frequently for 45–50 minutes. When both jams have almost thickened to desired consistency add watermelon jam to orange jam and simmer until thickened.

3   Remove from heat and stand 5 minutes. Pour into warm, sterilised jars and seal. When cool, label and date.

Above: Orange Watermelon Jam
Below: Melon and Peach Conserve

Nectarine Jam

As a summertime treat sandwich a sponge with Nectarine Jam and cream. Dust with icing sugar. Serve sponge with extra whipped cream and fresh nectarine slices.

PREPARATION TIME: *15 minutes*
COOKING TIME: *1¼ hours*
MAKES *1 litre*

1.5 kg firm ripe nectarines
juice and rind of 2 lemons,
1 cup water
6 cups sugar, warmed

1   Wash fruit and drain well. Halve, remove the stones and cut into thin slices. Tie stones in muslin bag.

2   Put fruit, stones, lemon juice and rind plus water into a large heavy based saucepan or boiler. Bring to boil and simmer until fruit is soft.

3   Stir through warmed sugar until sugar is dissolved. Increase heat and simmer until setting point is reached. Stir frequently as jam tends to catch.

4   Remove from heat and stand 5 minutes. Pour into warm, sterilised jars and seal immediately. When cool, label and date.

Black Cherry Jam

Top fruit flans with 1 cup of Black Cherry Jam for a delicious glaze. If jam is a little too stiff to spread, microwave with a small amount of water to a spreadable consistency. Cool before brushing over fruit.

PREPARATION TIME: *35 minutes plus*
overnight standing
COOKING TIME: *1½ hours*
MAKES *1 litre*

1 kg black cherries
juice 2 lemons
1 cup water
2 ½ cups sugar

1   Rinse cherries, drain well and remove stones. Put lemon juice and water into a bowl; add some of the sugar, then a layer of cherries. Continue this until sugar and cherries are used. Leave overnight.

2   Next day strain the syrup into a large saucepan or boiler and stir over medium heat until sugar has dissolved. Bring to boiling point, add cherries and boil for 45 minutes or until setting point is reached. Stir frequently to prevent catching.

3   Remove from heat and stand 5 minutes. Pour jam into warm, sterilised jars and seal immediately. When cool, label and date.

Peach and Ginger Jam

We used fresh and preserved ginger in this spicy jam.

PREPARATION TIME: *30 minutes*
COOKING TIME: *2 hours*
MAKES *2 litres*

3 kg peaches
60 g fresh green ginger
1 x 200 g pkt preserved ginger
1 cup water
juice 2 lemons
3 kg sugar, warmed

1   Peel and halve peaches and remove stones. Slice peaches and tie skins and stones in a piece of muslin. Finely chop the preserved ginger and grate fresh ginger.

2   Put peaches, fresh ginger, water and muslin bag into a large heavy based saucepan or boiler. Add lemon juice. Cover and simmer fruit gently until peaches are soft then remove muslin bag.

3   Add warmed sugar and preserved ginger and stir until sugar dissolves. Increase heat and boil rapidly, stirring frequently until jam reaches setting point.

4   Remove from heat and stand 1–2 minutes. Pour into warm, sterilised jars. When cool, label and date.

Caster sugar can be used to replace white crystal sugar, but the resulting preserve can be cloudy. The storage life is also reduced.

Fruits medium in acid content — blackberries (under-ripe), plums (ripe).

Peach and Ginger Jam and Black Cherry Jam

Clockwise from top: Peach and Passionfruit Jam, Tomato Jam, Honeydew and Pineapple Jam, and Peach and Passionfruit Jam in bowl

Peach and Passionfruit Jam

To peel large quantities of peaches, place in bowl, cover with boiling water and stand 1–2 minutes. Drain and cover with cold water. The skin should easily slip off.

PREPARATION TIME: *20 minutes plus overnight soaking*
COOKING TIME: *30 minutes*
MAKES *3 cups*

1 kg firm peaches
3 cups sugar
¼ cup lemon juice
½ cup passionfruit pulp

1 Peel and halve peaches and remove stones. Cut the flesh into thin slices, put into a dish and sprinkle with half the sugar. Cover and leave overnight.

2 Transfer to a pan, slowly bring to the boil, then simmer until peaches are just tender.

3 Warm the remaining sugar, add to the pan with the lemon juice and stir until the sugar has completely dissolved. Boil rapidly for 5 minutes then stir in the passionfruit pulp. Boil for another 7–10 minutes or until it gels when tested.

4 Ladle into warm, sterilised jars and seal airtight. When cool, label and date.

Honeydew and Pineapple Jam

Combine equal quantities of warmed Honeydew and Pineapple Jam with orange juice. Pour over a melon ball salad.

PREPARATION TIME: *20 minutes plus 2 hours standing*
COOKING TIME: *1–1½ hours*
MAKES *1.5 litres*

1 medium honeydew melon
1 medium pineapple
rind and juice of 2 lemons,
6 cups sugar, warmed
commercial pectin

1 Peel honeydew, remove the seeds and finely chop flesh. Peel, core and finely chop the pineapple. Add the rind and juice and stand at least 2 hours.

2 Put fruit into a large saucepan or boiler, and simmer until fruit is tender, about 20 minutes. Add commercial pectin (according to directions on packet).

3 Add the warmed sugar and stir until sugar has dissolved. Increase the heat and cook, stirring frequently until jam reaches setting point.

4 Remove from heat and stand 2 minutes. Pour into warm sterilised jars and seal. When cool, label and date.

Tomato Jam

Spread ½ cup warmed Tomato Jam over Swiss roll. Roll up and serve with favourite fruit coulis and cream. Add 2 tablespoons Tomato Jam to homemade tomato soup in winter.

PREPARATION TIME: *25 minutes*
COOKING TIME: *1 hour 5 minutes*
MAKES *1 litre*

1.5 kg tomatoes
100 g glacé pineapple
1 green apple
1 tablespoon grated lemon rind
½ cup lemon juice
3½ cups sugar

1 Peel and coarsely chop tomatoes. Coarsely chop pineapple. Peel, core and coarsely grate apple.

2 Combine tomatoes, pineapple, apple and rind in a large saucepan or boiler. Bring to the boil, simmer, uncovered, for about 20 minutes or until fruit is pulped. Stir in juice.

3 Add the warm sugar and stir until dissolved. Boil rapidly, uncovered, for about 45 minutes or until setting point is reached.

4 Remove jam from heat and stand 5 minutes. Pour into warm, sterilised jars and seal immediately. When cool, label and date.

Jams, marmalades, conserves, jellies can be stored for up to 18 months or eaten immediately.

A glut of fruit can be frozen for a short while until the time is available for making the preserves. The result will be only slightly inferior.

Blueberry and Apple Jelly

Apricot Butter

Apricots may be soaked in water overnight. Drain and discard water before puréeing. Apricot Butter may be used to make a delicious sauce. Mix Apricot Butter with natural yoghurt and a dash of soy sauce, heat gently and spoon over steamed chicken.

PREPARATION TIME: *10 minutes*
COOKING TIME: *20 minutes*
MAKES *2.5 litres*

200 g dried apricots
1 cup water
125 g butter
⅔ cup sugar
2 tablespoons lemon juice
3 eggs, lightly beaten

1   Combine apricots and water in saucepan, stirring until boiling. Reduce heat and simmer until water is absorbed. Purée in blender or food processor until smooth.

2   In basin or top of double saucepan, melt butter over barely simmering water. Add sugar and lemon juice; cook and stir for 2 minutes.

3   Add eggs all at once, cook, stirring constantly until mixture thickens and coats back of spoon. Thoroughly stir in purée.

4   Pour into warm, sterilised jars and seal. When cool, label and date. Store in a cool place and refrigerate after opening.

Blueberry and Apple Jelly

When buying blueberries look for firm, plump fruit with a blue-grey bloom. Blueberries do not ripen after picking, they only become softer. A delicious serving suggestion is to pan fry 4 flour-coated chicken breasts in pan. Remove and keep warm. Stir in half cup Blueberry and Apple Jelly to deglaze pan, simmer 1 minute, stir in ¼ cup cream. Pour over chicken to serve.

PREPARATION TIME: *20 minutes*
COOKING TIME: *1¾ hours*
MAKES *2.5 litres*

3 x 250 g punnets blueberries
6 medium green apples
4 medium pears
⅔ cup lemon juice
sugar

1   Wash blueberries, apples and pears then drain. Finely chop apples and pears including cores and seeds.

2   Combine blueberries with chopped fruit in a large saucepan or boiler and cover with water. Bring to boil and simmer, covered, for about 1 hour or until fruit is soft and pulpy.

3   Strain fruit and liquid through muslin bag suspended over a bowl for 3 hours. Measure juice and return to saucepan. Stir in lemon juice. Heat until boiling. Add ¾ cup sugar per cup of juice. Return to boil, stirring until sugar dissolves. Boil rapidly, uncovered, for about 40–45 minutes or until setting point is reached.

4   Remove cooked jelly from heat and stand 5 minutes. Pour into warm, sterilised jars and cool completely before sealing. When cool, label and date.

Fruit curds and butters may be enriched with orange flower water, rosewater and liqueurs for extra flavour and fragrance.

Fruit curds can be stored for up to 4 months. They are best kept in the refrigerator where possible, otherwise ensure seal is good and store in a very cool place.

Apricot Butter

Tropical Nut Jam

Fill a cooked pastry case with rum flavoured custard or cream and chill until custard firms. Spread top with Tropical Nut Jam.

PREPARATION TIME: *35 minutes*
COOKING TIME: *1¼ hours*
MAKES *1 litre*

2 medium, firm-ripe pineapples
½ cup water
185–250 g macadamia nuts
1 kg sugar, warmed

1   Peel and core enough pineapple to make 1 kg fruit. Use a food processor or coarsely chop the pulp; transfer with its juice to a large heavy saucepan or boiler; add water. Chop the macadamia nuts.

2   Heat pulp and nuts to boiling, reduce heat and simmer, stirring occasionally until fruit is tender and looks clear.

3   Add the warmed sugar and stir until dissolved. Continue cooking, stirring occasionally until setting point is reached.

4   Remove cooked jam from heat and stand 2 minutes. Pour into warm, sterilised jars and seal immediately. When cool, label and date.

The addition of nuts to a preserved mixture reduces the shelf life. The fat in the nuts becomes rancid, affecting the flavour. Use within 6 months of preparing.

Plum Jam

Serve Plum Jam spread on warm ginger pikelets or on wholemeal scones with dot of sour cream.

PREPARATION TIME: *20 minutes*
COOKING TIME: *1½ hours*
MAKES *1.5 litres*

1.25 kg plums
1 large green apple (250 g)
1.25 kg sugar
1¾ cups water
juice of 1 lemon

1   Wash, halve and stone plums. Wash, core and finely chop the apple.

2   Combine plums, apple, 1½ cups of the sugar and water. Cook gently, stirring occasionally until plums and apple are tender. Warm remaining sugar. Bring plums to the boil, add the warmed sugar and stir until dissolved. Add lemon juice and boil rapidly, stirring occasionally until fruit gels when tested, about 1 hour.

3   Ladle into warm, sterilised jars and seal. When cool, label and date.

Apricot Conserve

Top hot scones, brioches or croissants with Apricot Conserve or spread on bread for bread and butter custard.

PREPARATION TIME: *30 minutes*
COOKING TIME: *45 minutes*
MAKES *2 litres*

1.25 kg apricots
2 cups water
½ cup lemon juice
1.5 kg sugar, warmed

1   Halve apricots and remove and discard kernels; chop coarsely.

2   Combine apricots, water and lemon juice in large saucepan or boiler. Bring to the boil and boil slowly, covered for 10 minutes.

3   Add the warmed sugar and stir until dissolved. Boil rapidly, uncovered until setting point is reached.

4   Remove conserve from heat and stand 10 minutes. Pour into warm, sterilised jars. Seal when cold. Label and date.

Apricot Conserve, Tropical Nut Jam and Plum Jam

SUMMER PICKLES

Spiced Peaches
21

Garlic Peppers
21

Cucumber and Onion Relish
21

Peperonata
22

Cucumber Relish
22

Tomato Pickle
22

Bread and Butter Cucumbers
25

Cucumber Wedges with Dill
25

Spiced Peaches

Peaches must lie packed very tightly to prevent them from floating. Top peaches will not be covered in syrup if this occurs. Place Spiced Peaches in chafing dish or frypan and flame with brandy. Serve over vanilla ice-cream topped with roasted flaked almonds.

PREPARATION TIME: *1 hour*
COOKING TIME: *7–10 minutes*
MAKES *1.5 litres*

1 kg peaches
2 cups sugar
2 cups water
1 whole vanilla bean
1 cinnamon stick
8 whole coriander seeds
1 teaspoon whole cloves
strips of rind from 1 lemon

1   Prepare peaches by blanching, skinning and removing stones. Cut in halves or quarters. Pack prepared peaches into sterilised jars.

2   Place sugar in heavy based saucepan or boiler and add water. Stir over low heat until sugar is dissolved. Add spices and lemon rind. Bring to the boil, reduce heat and simmer for 6–8 minutes.

3   Strain syrup and reserve vanilla bean. Pour syrup over peaches and place vanilla bean in jar, with peaches and syrup. Seal. When cool, label and date.

Garlic Peppers

Use capsicums that are at their freshest seasonal best. They should be well shaped, thick skinned and deeply coloured. They store well for up to 6 months. Cut into thin strips and add to stir-fried vegetables. Chop finely and add to mayonnaise. Serve as an accompaniment to fried fish.

PREPARATION TIME: *15 minutes*
COOKING TIME: *15 minutes*
MAKES *1 litre*

1 green capsicum
1 red capsicum
2 cloves garlic, peeled and cut into slices
½ cup sugar
2 cups white wine vinegar
2 teaspoons salt

1   Cut capsicums lengthwise into quarters. Discard core, seeds and white pith. Blanch in boiling water until softened, about 1 minute. Drain and pack snugly into jar with prepared garlic.

2   In saucepan slowly heat sugar, vinegar and salt, stirring until sugar dissolves. Heat until boiling.

3   Pour hot liquid over capsicums. Cover at once with airtight lid. Label and date. Mature 1 week before opening.

Cucumber and Onion Relish

This quick and easy relish needs no cooking. Store in the refrigerator. Cucumber and Onion Relish is a great sandwich filling. To make a spicy dip, drain, combine with sour cream and mayonnaise and serve with corn chips, crackers and fresh vegetable sticks.

PREPARATION TIME: *30 minutes*
COOKING TIME: *Nil*
MAKES *about 3½ cups*

1 cucumber
4 small onions, finely chopped
2 small red chillies, finely chopped
1 cup white vinegar
¼ cup sugar
6 whole berries allspice
¼ cup finely chopped fresh mint

1   Peel cucumber, halve lengthwise. Remove and discard seeds.

2   Combine cucumber, onion and chillies in large bowl and cover with water. Cover, refrigerate for several hours then drain.

3   Combine cucumber mixture with remaining ingredients; mix well. Pack into warm, sterilised jars. Refrigerate for a few days before serving.

Handle chillies with care. Best to use disposable plastic gloves when preparing, or chop in a blender. If hands do come into contact with chillies, avoid touching face area or tender skin, since burning will result.

Do not prepare fruit or vegetables with a steel knife since this discolours the produce and taints the flavour.

Peperonata

Marvellous served as part of an antipasto platter, tossed into a green salad, or spooned into a sautéed chicken dish just before serving. Store in the refrigerator.

PREPARATION TIME: *30 minutes*
COOKING TIME: *1 hour*
MAKES *1.5 litres*

4 large onions, thickly sliced
½ cup vegetable oil
5 red capsicums, seeded, cut into strips
½ cup water
½ cup chopped parsley
4 cloves garlic, sliced
1 tablespoon sugar
2 tablespoons drained capers
2 tablespoons white vinegar

1   Cook onions in hot oil in a large heavy based saucepan or boiler until soft. Add capsicums and water.

2   Simmer gently, stirring occasionally, until capsicums are soft, 20 minutes.

3   Add parsley, garlic, sugar, capers and vinegar. Heat until boiling, reduce heat and simmer until thick, 15 minutes.

4   Cool slightly then spoon into warm, sterilised jars and seal.

Cucumber Relish

Serve Cucumber Relish with poached or steamed fish.

PREPARATION TIME: *15 minutes*
plus overnight standing
COOKING TIME: *1 hour*
MAKES *1 litre*

1 kg yellow apple cucumbers
2 small cucumbers
2 tablespoons salt
1 red capsicum
1 green capsicum
310 g can corn kernels, drained
1 onion, chopped
2 teaspoons celery seeds
2 teaspoons brown mustard seeds
1 cup white vinegar
1½ cups sugar

Pickling is an ancient method of preserving. The Romans pickled fruit from the Middle East and Africa, and made relishes of herbs, seeds, roots, flowers and vegetables in oil, brine and vinegars.

1   Slice cucumbers thinly. Place in a large bowl, sprinkle with salt, cover with dry cloth and stand overnight. Dice capsicums and onion and chop finely. Drain cucumbers, rinse in cold water then drain again.

2   Place all ingredients in a large saucepan or boiler. Bring to boil, and simmer for 1 hour or until mixture is thick, stirring occasionally.

3   Remove from heat. Spoon into warm, sterilised jars and seal. When cool, label and date.

Tomato Pickle

Tomato Pickle is a zesty condiment for cold meats. Serve with cheese and bread.

PREPARATION TIME: *1 hour*
plus overnight standing
COOKING TIME: *8 minutes*
MAKES *3½ cups*

2 kg green tomatoes
1 kg onions
1 medium cucumber
2 litres water
¾ cup salt
2 cups firmly packed brown sugar
1½ teaspoons dry mustard
2 teaspoons turmeric
1 teaspoon curry powder
¼ teaspoon cayenne pepper
½ cup plain flour
2 cups malt vinegar

1   Chop tomatoes. Peel and chop onions and cucumber. Place vegetables in large bowl, add water and sprinkle with salt. Stand overnight.

2   Place vegetables and brine in large saucepan or boiler. Bring to the boil and boil for 3 minutes; drain.

3   Return vegetables to saucepan; add sugar, mustard, turmeric, curry powder and pepper. Blend flour with vinegar, add to pan and bring to the boil. Simmer for 5 minutes, stirring constantly.

4   Remove from heat, pour into warm, sterilised jars and seal. When cool, label and date.

Clockwise from top: Tomato Pickle, Cucumber Relish and Peperonata served with spatchcocks

Cucumber Wedges with Dill

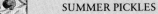

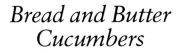

Bread and Butter Cucumbers

The long, thin-skinned cucumbers are best used for this recipe. Serve drained Bread and Butter Cucumbers with salads or add to sandwich fillings or dips.

PREPARATION TIME: *30 minutes plus overnight standing*
COOKING TIME: *10 minutes*
MAKES *2 litres*

3 cucumbers
salt
2 cups white vinegar
3 tablespoons sugar
½ cup hot water
2 teaspoons salt
2 teaspoons mustard seeds
1 red capsicum, thinly sliced

1   Cut washed, unpeeled cucumbers into very thin slices. Layer cucumbers in large bowl and sprinkle lightly with salt between layers. Cover and stand overnight.

2   Rinse cucumbers under cold water; drain well. Place vinegar, sugar, hot water, salt and mustard seeds in large saucepan or boiler. Bring to the boil, stirring until sugar is dissolved. Simmer, uncovered, for 5 minutes.

3   Add cucumber slices to pan and bring to the boil. Remove from heat.

4   Using tongs, pack cucumber slices into warm, sterilised jars. Add a few strips of capsicum to each jar. Pour hot vinegar mixture into jars to cover cucumbers. Seal. When cool, label and date.

Cucumber Wedges with Dill

Drain cucumbers and chop finely. Combine with thick plain natural yoghurt and crushed garlic, and serve as a dip with cracker biscuits.

PREPARATION TIME: *10 minutes plus overnight standing*
COOKING TIME: *5 minutes*
MAKES *2.5 litres*

4 large cucumbers
2 onions
2 tablespoons salt
¾ cup sugar
3 cups white vinegar
1 teaspoon black mustard seeds
1 tablespoon currants
6 red chillies
10 sprigs dill

1   Coarsely chop cucumbers and thinly slice onions. Place cucumber and onions in bowl, sprinkle with salt, cover with dry cloth and stand overnight. Rinse and drain vegetables.

2   Combine sugar, vinegar and seeds in saucepan, bring slowly to boil and simmer 5 minutes.

3   Pack cucumbers, onions, currants, chillies and dill into warm, sterilised jars. Pour boiling liquid over vegetables and seal. When cool, label and date.

Bread and Butter Cucumbers

SUMMER CHUTNEYS

Apricot and Passionfruit Chutney
27

Chilli Plum Sauce
27

Plum and Mint Sauce
27

Plum Cardamom Chutney
28

Tomato Peach Relish
28

Westmoreland Chutney
28

Tomato Chutney
30

Ginger Peach Relish
30

Apricot Chutney
31

Sweetcorn Relish
31

Plum and Pineapple Chutney
32

Tomato Sauce
32

Apricot and Passionfruit Chutney

This chutney can be used to make a tasty dip. Combine ½ cup Apricot and Passionfruit Chutney with 250 g ricotta cheese. Serve with crudités or rice crackers.

PREPARATION TIME: *45 minutes*
COOKING TIME: *2 hours*
MAKES *1 litre*

1 kg ripe firm apricots
2 tablespoons grated fresh ginger
1 tablespoon dry mustard
2 teaspoons salt
1 cup passionfruit pulp (about 10 passionfruit)
500 g onions, chopped finely
½ teaspoon nutmeg
1½ cups brown sugar
2½ cups white vinegar

1   Wash apricots and drain well. Halve the apricots, stone and chop coarsely.

2   Put all ingredients except vinegar into a saucepan or boiler, add half the vinegar and bring to boiling point, stirring until sugar has dissolved. Simmer for 10 minutes and stir in remaining vinegar. Bring to boiling point, reduce heat and cook gently 1¼–1¾ hours or until thick.

3   Pour into warm, sterilised jars and seal airtight. When cool, label and date.

Chilli Plum Sauce

Serve with marinated chicken wings, Chinese egg rolls, dim sims, and barbecued meats.

PREPARATION TIME: *1 hour*
COOKING TIME: *2–2½ hours*
MAKES *3 litres*

2 kg ripe red plums
1.5 kg onions
4 fresh red chillies
1½ cups sultanas
50 g fresh green ginger, grated
1.25 litres white wine vinegar
3 cups brown sugar

1 tablespoon salt
3 teaspoons dry mustard
1 teaspoon ground allspice
1 teaspoon nutmeg
½ teaspoon ground turmeric

1   Wash, halve, stone and coarsely chop plums. Finely chop onions. Seed and finely chop chillies.

2   In a large saucepan or boiler, combine plums, onions, chillies, sultanas and ginger. Add 3 cups of vinegar. Heat to boiling, reduce heat and simmer, stirring occasionally, for 40 minutes. Blend mixture in blender or purée in food processor. Return to clean boiler. Add remaining vinegar, sugar, salt, mustard, allspice, nutmeg and turmeric. Heat to boiling, reduce and simmer, stirring occasionally until a thick sauce consistency, about 1½ hours.

3   Cool slightly; pour into hot clean jars or bottles and seal. When cool, label and date. Refrigerate after opening.

Plum and Mint Sauce

Serve hot with roast lamb.

PREPARATION TIME: *30 minutes*
COOKING TIME: *45 minutes*
MAKES *1.25 litres*

1.5 kg dark red plums
1¼ cups white wine vinegar
1¼ cups malt vinegar
1 cup sugar
1 teaspoon dry mustard
2 teaspoons salt
2 tablespoons mint chopped finely

1   Wash, halve and stone the plums, chop coarsely.

2   Put all ingredients except mint into a large saucepan or boiler and bring to boiling point, stirring until sugar dissolves. Reduce heat and simmer until plums are soft and mixture has thickened slightly, about 35 minutes. Remove from heat and cool slightly. Blend or purée, add mint and simmer another 10 minutes.

3   Pour into warm, sterilised jars and seal. When cool, label and date.

Chutneys originated in India, where they are served to stimulate appetite and aid digestion. Indians believe a good chutney is so hot and spicy you can hardly eat it, yet so sweet you cannot resist it.

Chutneys can be stored for up to 2 years. They are best kept for at least 1 month prior to using.

Plum Cardamom Chutney

Dark red plums are best used for this recipe. Use to accompany cold meats, meat loaves and meat patties.

PREPARATION TIME: *35 minutes*
COOKING TIME: *1½–2 hours*
MAKES *2 litres*

500 g green apples
500 g onions
1 kg plums
250 g sultanas
1 tablespoon salt
½ teaspoon ground allspice
¼ teaspoon ground cloves
½ teaspoon dry mustard
1 teaspoon ground cardamom
1¼ cups brown sugar
1 litre malt vinegar

1   Peel, core and finely chop the apples, peel and finely chop the onions. Wash, stone, and coarsely chop the plums; chop sultanas in half.

2   Put all the ingredients into a large saucepan or boiler and bring to boiling point, stirring until sugar is dissolved. Reduce heat and simmer gently, stirring occasionally for 1½–2 hours or until thick.

3   Turn into warm, sterilised jars and seal. When cool, label and date.

Tomato Peach Relish

Replace peaches with nectarines, plums or any seasonal stone fruit.

PREPARATION TIME: *45 minutes*
COOKING TIME: *1½–2 hours*
MAKES *2 litres*

1.25 kg peaches
500 g onions
1.5 kg ripe tomatoes, peeled and chopped
2 teaspoons whole black peppercorns
1 teaspoon ground allspice
2 tablespoons grated fresh ginger

2 teaspoons mustard seeds
3 bay leaves
1 large clove garlic
1½ cups sultanas
1 teaspoon very finely chopped red chilli
2½ cups brown sugar
1 teaspoon salt
1½ cups white vinegar

1   Peel and stone the peaches and chop coarsely; finely chop onions.

2   Put all ingredients into a large saucepan or boiler and bring to the boil, stirring occasionally. Reduce heat and simmer, stirring frequently for 1½–2 hours or until thick.

3   Spoon the relish into warm, sterilised jars and seal airtight. When cool, label and date.

Westmoreland Chutney

Serve Westmoreland Chutney with cold meats, corned meat, terrines, meat loaves, pickled pork or continental sausages.

PREPARATION TIME: *40 minutes*
COOKING TIME: *2½ hours*
MAKES *1.5 litres*

1½ kg plums
500 g zucchini
500 g onions
1½ cups sultanas
4 cups brown sugar
1 litre malt vinegar
2 teaspoons ground ginger
1 teaspoon dry mustard

1   Wash, stone and chop the plums coarsely; finely chop zucchini, peel and finely chop the onions.

2   Put all ingredients except vinegar into a large saucepan or boiler. Add half the vinegar. Cook gently, stirring frequently for 30 minutes. Add remaining vinegar and simmer gently for another 2 hours or until thick.

3   Turn into warm, sterilised jars and seal. When cool, label and date.

Fruits low in acid content — apricots, blackberries (ripe), cherries (sweet or ripe), marrow, melons, peaches, pears, raspberries, strawberries.

In the early nineteenth century silver cruet sets, including glass bottles for serving sauces and chutneys, were introduced to British dining tables. Because of the popularity of these condiments, cruet sets soon become standard utensils on every table.

Clockwise from top: Tomato and Peach Relish and Westmoreland Chutney served with terrine, Plum Cardamom Chutney served with ham, and Tomato Peach Relish in bowl

For a spicy fragrant vinaigrette or salad dressing add 2–3 tablespoons of your favourite relish or chutney to the oil and vinegar base. Shake well just before serving.

Ginger Peach Relish

Ginger Peach Relish

Ginger Peach Relish is a delicious accompaniment to lamb chops or lamb roast, ham, corned beef and cold meats of various kinds.

PREPARATION TIME: *15 minutes*
COOKING TIME: *20 minutes*
MAKES *about 1 litre*

6 large ripe peaches
1 tablespoon finely chopped preserved ginger
2 tablespoons brown sugar
2 tablespoons vinegar
2 teaspoons soy sauce

1   Place peaches in large bowl and cover with boiling water. Stand 1 minute, drain, then carefully remove skins from peaches. Halve peaches, discard stones and chop coarsely.

2   Combine peaches with remaining ingredients in large saucepan or boiler. Bring to the boil and simmer, covered, for 15 minutes. Stir occasionally with wooden spoon, breaking up peaches with spoon until soft and pulpy.

3   Spoon into warm, sterilised jars and seal. When cool, label and date. Refrigerate until required.

Tomato Chutney

Combine 1 cup Tomato Chutney with 250 g creamed ricotta cheese and 1 small can pink salmon, mashed; serve either as a spread for plain biscuits, a dip, or set with gelatine as a terrine.

PREPARATION TIME: *30 minutes*
COOKING TIME: *2 hours*
MAKES *1.5 litres*

1 kg ripe tomatoes
3 onions
2 green apples
3 white-fleshed peaches
2 ¾ cups dark brown sugar
2 cups white vinegar
1 tablespoon salt
1 teaspoon mixed spice
1 teaspoon Mexican chilli powder

1   Peel and coarsely chop tomatoes, onions and apples. Peel, halve and stone peaches, and chop coarsely.

2   Place all ingredients in a large saucepan or boiler. Bring slowly to boil and simmer, uncovered, for about 2 hours or until mixture is thick, stirring occasionally.

3   Remove chutney from the heat and stand 5 minutes. Spoon into warm sterilised jars and seal immediately. When cool, label and date.

Apricot Chutney

Combine 3 tablespoons Apricot Chutney with 1 cup grated tasty cheese. Spread on lightly toasted bread and place under hot grill until melted and browned. Cut into fingers and serve.

PREPARATION TIME: *20 minutes*
COOKING TIME: *1½ hours*
MAKES *1.5 litres*

1.5 kg apricots, stoned
3 medium onions, finely chopped
1½ cups raisins, chopped
2 cups brown sugar
1 tablespoon mustard seeds
½ teaspoon chilli powder
2 cups malt vinegar
½ teaspoon cinnamon
1 teaspoon turmeric
1 orange, juice and rind
1 lemon, juice and rind
¼ cup slivered almonds

1   Place all ingredients except almonds in large heavy based saucepan or boiler. Bring to boil, reduce heat and simmer until soft and pulpy. Stir occasionally to prevent sticking. Stir in almonds.

2   Pour into warm, sterilised jars and seal airtight. When cool, label and date.

Sweetcorn Relish

Fresh or canned sweetcorn kernels may be used for this spicy relish. If you prefer a less sharp flavour, replace ½ cup of the vinegar with water. Blend together ½ cup Sweetcorn Relish with 250 g softened cream cheese and serve as a dip with crisp celery and carrot sticks, or plain biscuits.

PREPARATION TIME: *15 minutes*
COOKING TIME: *20 minutes*
MAKES *1 litre*

1 tablespoon cornflour
1½ cups white wine vinegar
1 large onion, chopped
1 clove garlic, crushed
1 tablespoon vegetable oil
1 red capsicum, chopped
375 g sweetcorn kernels
⅓ cup sugar
1 tablespoon dry mustard
2 teaspoons turmeric
½ teaspoon ground pepper

1   Blend cornflour with a little of the vinegar until smooth.

2   In a large saucepan cook onion and garlic in oil until softened, add capsicums, remaining vinegar, corn, sugar, mustard and turmeric. Heat, stirring, until boiling.

3   Remove from heat. Stir in the cornflour mixture. Simmer, stirring for about 10 minutes. Stir in pepper.

4   Remove from heat, pour into warm, sterilised jars and seal. When cool, label and date.

Microwave Method
Prepare through end of step 1, step 2; Heat oil in large bowl at High power for 1 minute. Add capsicums, onions, garlic, only 1 cup of vinegar, corn, sugar, mustard and turmeric. Cook 2 minutes. Reduce to Low power, cook 4 minutes then stir in cornflour mixture. Cook at High power for 4–6 minutes more, stirring every minute. Add pepper.

Wear thick cotton gloves when bottling preserves to avoid burns from splashed preserves. They also allow you to handle bottles without burning hands.

If using spices in chutneys, jams, jellies or pickles, tie in muslin so they can be found and removed prior to bottling.

Plum and Pineapple Chutney

Serve Plum and Pineapple Chutney with game, pork or corned meats. Combine ¾ cup Chutney with 3 cups fresh bread-crumbs and 1 egg yolk. Use as a seasoning in a rolled pork loin.

PREPARATION TIME: *45 minutes*
COOKING TIME: *2 hours*
MAKES *1.5 litres*

1 kg red plums
1 large pineapple
500 g onions
375 g raisins
1 cup brown sugar
2 tablespoons very finely chopped fresh ginger root
1 teaspoon ground allspice
½ teaspoon coarsely ground black pepper
½ teaspoon dry mustard
½ teaspoon nutmeg
1 tablespoon salt
1¼ cups malt vinegar

1 Wash plums, stone and chop coarsely. Peel pineapple and chop finely. Chop onions finely; chop raisins coarsely.

2 Put all the ingredients except vinegar into a large saucepan and stir over a low heat 3–4 minutes. Add half the vinegar and simmer for about 20 minutes, stirring occasionally. Add the rest of the vinegar and continue cooking gently another 1½ hours or until thick.

3 Turn into warm, sterilised jars and seal. When cool, label and date.

Sweetcorn Relish and Plum and Pineapple Chutney

Tomato Sauce

Our version of the all-time favourite Tomato Sauce is rich and tasty. It's the perfect ingredient for marinades. You can add ¼ cup to a meatloaf mixture, or add to mayonnaise to make tangy cocktail sauce.

PREPARATION TIME: *30 minutes*
COOKING TIME: *1½ hours*
MAKES *2 litres*

2 kg ripe tomatoes
3 green apples
3 onions
2½ cups malt vinegar
1 clove garlic, crushed
2 cups sugar
2 tablespoons salt
½ teaspoon cayenne pepper
1 teaspoon whole cloves
1 teaspoon whole allspice

1 Peel tomatoes and chop coarsely. Peel and core apples and peel onions. Coarsely chop apples and onions.

2 Combine tomatoes, apples, onions, vinegar and garlic in large saucepan or boiler. Bring to the boil and simmer, uncovered, for 1 hour. Push mixture through sieve.

3 Return sieved mixture to saucepan with sugar, salt and cayenne. Tie cloves and allspice in a piece of muslin and add to pan. Bring to the boil and simmer for about 30 minutes or until sauce has thickened slightly.

4 Remove muslin bag from pan and pour sauce into warm, sterilised jars or bottles and seal immediately. When cool, label and date.

Tomato Sauce

JAM MAKING

Jam is made by boiling together sugar and fruit to form a sugar concentration high enough to preserve the mixture and prevent spoilage. While jam doesn't store indefinitely it usually has a shelf life of about two years unless the sugar concentration is not high enough. In this case the jam will become mouldy sooner.

A good jam should be set to a firm consistency and have a good clear colour, characteristic of the fruit in the jam. The flavour should be that of the fruit without tasting excessively sweet or acidic. What makes jam set is the combination of sugar, pectin and acid; the latter two are both naturally occurring in fruit but to varying degrees. It is for this reason that some fruits are combined with other fruits or commercial preparations to produce a balance that will give a good setting quality.

STAGES IN JAM MAKING

First Stage Fruit preparation. The choice of fruit will have a large bearing on the result. Choose fruit that is slightly under-ripe; this has the highest pectin, sugar and acid ratio. Remove any leaves and stalks and cut off any bruised or damaged sections of the fruit. Fruit should be washed under cold running water and patted dry with a clean cloth or kitchen paper. When patting fruit dry, be careful not to damage the fruit, particularly soft fruits such as berries. Fruit should be peeled, cut or sliced as the recipe suggests; however it is best if this is done at the last minute to prevent the fruit discolouring.

The Second Stage Releasing the pectin from the fruit. This is done by cooking and sometimes soaking the fruit in water. The acid present in the fruit assists in releasing the pectin into the water and is done prior to adding the sugar. The time this takes will vary according to the type of fruit used and the pectin and acid balance. It is important at this stage that the fruit is soft, since the sugar has a tendency to make the fruit firm.

Testing for Pectin Content At this stage it is a good idea to test the mixture for the pectin content. Fruit that is over-ripe will have a low pectin content and should not be used where possible. Fruit that is slightly under-ripe gives the highest balance of pectin and acid.

To Test After boiling mixture until fruit is soft, remove a teaspoon of liquid from the pan, allow to cool and place in a small container such as an egg cup or small glass. Add about 3 teaspoons methylated spirits and stand mixture for about 3 minutes. When the pectin content is high, the juice will form a clear jelly-like clump. If the jelly breaks into pieces or a mixture with only a few lumps, the pectin content will not be sufficient to set the jam. Often if the mixture is boiled longer then more pectin will be released; however if the fruit is low in pectin then a little commercial pectin may need to be added. Sometimes fruits low in pectin are combined with fruit or fruit juices that are high in pectin to avoid this. If the fruit is slightly under-ripe, in good condition and a reliable recipe is used then there really is no reason to test the pectin content.

3 Place a teaspoon of fruit pulp in a small glass and add methylated spirits; pulp should begin to gel.

1 Wash, peel and chop fruit. Remove and discard any leaves, stalks and bruised sections of fruit.

2 Place fruit in a large saucepan or boiler, bring to the boil, reduce heat and simmer until fruit is soft.

The Third Stage Cooking with the addition of sugar. For best results, the sugar should be warmed by placing in a low oven until warm. It is not absolutely necessary to warm the sugar prior to adding to the fruit mixture; however the amount of scum that forms on the surface is kept to a minimum. Once the sugar has been added the jam is boiled rapidly to increase the concentration of sugar. When the correct concentration of sugar is reached, the jam has reached its setting point and at this stage is placed in jars for storing.

4 Place sugar in a baking tray, heat in a moderately slow oven until sugar is just warm. Add warmed sugar to pulp.

Tests for setting point

It is necessary to test hot jam mixtures to ensure the setting point has been reached. There are several methods by which this can be done. The most reliable method is using a sugar thermometer. When the thermometer registers 105°C the jam is ready. The concentration of sugar will be high enough to prevent spoilage and the jam should set to a firm gel.

The saucer test is the most commonly used method for testing jam. A saucer is placed in the freezer to become very cold. Place a little jam on the plate and leave it undisturbed to become cold. Use a spoon or your finger and gently push the jam slightly. If the surface appears a little wrinkly with a skin on the surface, the jam is ready. If the jam is still runny, continue to boil mixture until setting point is reached.

5 Use a sugar thermometer to test if setting point is reached; when the thermometer reaches 105°C, jam is ready.

Bottling

Before bottling jam, spoon off any scum from the surface of the jam with a metal spoon. Allow jam to stand 5 minutes prior to bottling to prevent the fruit sinking to the base of the jar.

6 Using a metal spoon, lift off any scum that may have formed over the surface of the jam.

CONSERVES

Conserves are very similiar to jams except that the fruit remains firm, retaining its original shape. This is achieved by only partially softening the fruit before adding the sugar. The sugar keeps the fruit firm during cooking, so giving the appearance of fruit suspended in a light jam mixture. Conserves are a particularly suitable treatment for soft fruits such as apricots, peaches and berry fruits. The steps involved are the same as for jam making, only the softening of the fruit being shorter as mentioned above.

1 Wash fruit and remove stalks. Place fruit in a bowl with sugar. Cover and stand overnight.

2 Using a fine strainer, gently strain liquid from fruit, taking care not to bruise fruit.

3 Combine liquid and sugar in a large saucepan or boiler, and stir over low heat until sugar dissolves.

4 Add fruit to the saucepan, continue cooking until setting point is reached.

5 To test setting point, place a little jam syrup on a cold saucer. When cold, push jam slightly — it should wrinkle.

6 Carefully ladle into warm sterilised jars. When cool, seal and label.

MARMALADES

Marmalades are essentially citrus jams and are made by the same method as other fruit jams. When cooking marmalades the initial softening of the fruit takes longer than in most jams, owing to the rind of citrus fruit being tougher than fruit pulp. Because of the long initial cooking usually extra water is added to compensate for the extra evaporation.

The cutting of citrus fruit is time-consuming. However, this can be minimised by the use of a food processor or vegetable slicer.

Because of the high acid and pectin content of citrus fruits, it is not normally necessary to test the mixture for pectin during the initial stages of cooking.

1 Slice citrus fruits thinly. Place fruit and water in a large bowl. Cover and stand overnight.

2 Place fruit and water in a large saucepan or boiler. Bring to the boil and simmer until citrus rind softens.

3 Add warmed sugar to saucepan, stirring until sugar dissolves.

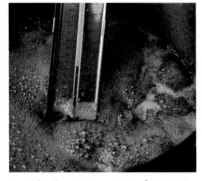

4 Check setting point by testing marmalade with a sugar thermometer. Setting point is 105°C.

5 Carefully pour marmalade into sterilised jars, using cotton gloves to hold jars as they become very hot.

6 To seal, carefully pour melted wax over marmalade. When cool, label and date.

Autumn

Autumn's harvest gives us crisp, full flavoured apples, ripe juicy pears, exotic fruits that include guava and passionfruit, all ideal for jam, pickle and chutney making. Now is the time to look to the freshly dried vine and tree fruits also perfect for preserving. Try our luscious Fig Butter, Fruit Fiesta Conserve or spicy Fruity Relish.

Clockwise from top: Fig Butter, Fruit Fiesta Conserve and Tomato Passionfruit Jam

AUTUMN JAMS

Tomato Passionfruit Jam
41

Fig Butter
41

Fruit Fiesta Conserve
41

Dried Fig Jam
43

Apricot Pineapple Jam
43

Lemon Passionfruit Butter
43

Passionfruit Banana Cream
45

Guava Jelly
45

Sage Jelly
45

Rosemary, Tomato and Apple Jelly
46

Apple Passionfruit Jam
46

Tomato Passionfruit Jam

Unroll freshly baked cool Swiss roll. Whip 300 mL sour cream until fluffy. Fold through ½ cup Tomato Passionfruit Jam. Spread over Swiss roll and reroll. Serve with extra cream and fresh passionfruit.

PREPARATION TIME: *20 minutes*
COOKING TIME: *1½ hours*
MAKES *1 litre*

1 kg firm ripe tomatoes
10 passionfruit (¾ cup pulp)
1.25 kg sugar, warmed

1 Wash, peel and coarsely chop tomatoes. Remove pulp from passionfruit and put half the skins into a saucepan, add enough water to cover and cook briskly 20 minutes or until skins are soft inside. Using a teaspoon, scoop out all the softened white inner skin, put this aside and discard the outer skins.

2 Put tomatoes and passionfruit pulp into a large saucepan or boiler and bring to boiling point.

3 Add the scrapings from the skins and the warmed sugar and stir until sugar has dissolved. Boil rapidly, stirring frequently until setting point is reached.

4 Remove cooked jam from heat and stand 1–2 minutes. Pour into warm, sterilised jars and seal immediately. When cool, label and date.

Fig Butter

Use as filling for filo pastry rolls or triangles. Add chopped pistachio nuts for taste and texture.

PREPARATION TIME: *30 minutes*
COOKING TIME: *15 minutes*
MAKES *3 cups*

375 g dried figs, stems removed
1 cup orange juice
1 cup water

1 small lemon, chopped (do not peel)
½ cup brown sugar
3 teaspoons rose or orange- flower water

1 Place figs, orange juice, water and lemon in a saucepan, bring to the boil. Reduce heat and simmer until figs are tender.

2 Allow to cool, then place in blender or food processor and process until smooth. Return to saucepan and stir in sugar. Stir over low heat until mixture is thick enough to spread, about 10 minutes. Stir through rose or orange water.

3 Spoon into warm, sterilised jars and seal. Label and date.

Fruit Fiesta Conserve

This delightful conserve is an attractive filling for small tartlets.

PREPARATION TIME: *30 minutes plus overnight standing*
COOKING TIME: *1½ hours*
MAKES *4 litres*

250 g dried apricots
250 g dried apples
250 g dried peaches
125 g dried figs
125 g glacé pineapple
125 g glacé cherries
3 litres water
2 kg sugar, warmed
juice of 3 large lemons (about 6 tablespoons)
3 tablespoons orange flavoured liqueur

1 Roughly chop the fruits, cover with water and stand overnight.

2 Transfer the fruit to large heavy saucepan or boiler and bring to the boil. Add the warmed sugar and stir until dissolved.

3 Reduce heat and simmer for 30 minutes. Add the lemon juice and simmer until conserve gels when tested. Remove from heat, add the liqueur and stir well.

4 Leave for 30 minutes, stir again, then spoon into warm, sterilised jars and seal. When cool, label and date.

If jam doesn't set after cooling in jars, return to the pan and continue cooking until setting point is reached. The keeping quality will be affected so use as soon as possible.

Ensure fruit is well washed when making jellies, avoiding a dirty, cloudy appearance.

Lemon Passion Butter in bowl, Apricot Pineapple Jam and Dried Fig Jam on plate

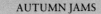

Dried Fig Jam

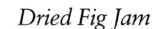

Spoon Fig Jam into small pastry cases and ice with lemon icing; serve as an afternoon tea treat.

PREPARATION TIME: *10 minutes plus overnight soaking*
COOKING TIME: *1 hour*
MAKES *1 litre*

500 g dried figs
1 litre water
⅓ cup lemon juice
3 cups sugar, warmed
1 teaspoon grated lemon rind

1   Chop the figs coarsely, put into a bowl, pour over the water and stand overnight.

2   Next day, transfer the figs and water to a saucepan. Bring to boiling point, reduce heat, cover and cook gently until the figs are tender.

3   Add the lemon juice, warmed sugar and grated lemon rind and stir over low heat until the sugar has dissolved. Bring to boiling point and boil steadily, stirring occasionally until it gels when tested.

4   Ladle into warm, sterilised jars and seal. When cool, label and date.

Apricot Pineapple Jam

Fill tartlet cases with Apricot and Pineapple Jam. Top with cream. Apricot and Pineapple Jam can also be used as a baste on roast meats by mixing ¼ cup jam with ¼ cup orange juice, a dash of soy sauce and chopped mint.

PREPARATION TIME: *20 minutes plus 4–6 hours soaking time*
COOKING TIME: *1 hour*
MAKES *1.5 litres*

250 g dried apricots
3 ¾ cups hot water
1 ½ cups finely chopped fresh pineapple
1 tablespoon lemon juice
4 cups sugar, warmed

1   Put apricots into a bowl, add the hot water and stand for 4–6 hours.

2   Pour apricots and liquid into a saucepan, add the grated pineapple and bring to boiling point. Reduce heat and simmer until apricots are tender.

3   Stir in the lemon juice, then add the warmed sugar and stir until sugar has dissolved. Cook gently until it gels when tested.

4   Pour into warm, sterilised jars and seal. When cool, label and date.

Lemon Passion Butter

Blend ½ cup Lemon Passion Butter with 1 cup Ricotta cheese until smooth. Using a sorbet scoop, scoop 3 balls of mixture onto each plate. Serve with raspberry purée for a light and refreshing dessert.

PREPARATION TIME: *15 minutes*
COOKING TIME: *20 minutes*
MAKES *1.5 litres*

250 g butter
1½ cups sugar
1 tablespoon finely grated lemon rind
1 cup lemon juice
pulp of 4 passionfruit
8 eggs, lightly beaten

1   Chop butter into 2 cm cubes.

2   Combine all ingredients in a large heatproof bowl. Stir constantly over pan of simmering water for about 20 minutes or until mixture coats the back of a metal spoon.

3   Remove cooked butter from the heat and stand 2 minutes. Pour into warm, sterilised jars and seal immediately. When cool, label and date. Refrigerate butter after opening.

For the best flavour use unsalted butter in fruit curds. If you wish to reduce the cholesterol content it is possible to substitute polyunsaturated margarine. The result will be slightly oilier.

Fresh seasonal figs are delicious. They need no preparation and are best served at room temperature. Figs have a very thin skin and should be handled with care. They are classified by the colour of their skins: purple, white, black and red. Pear or egg shaped, figs contain a soft, juicy red flesh full of tiny edible seeds.

Clockwise from top left: Guava Jelly, Rosemary, Tomato and Apple Jelly and Sage Jelly

Passionfruit Banana Cream

Fold ¼ cup Passionfruit Banana Cream through whipped cream for a topping for fruit salad or ice-cream.

PREPARATION TIME: *15 minutes*
COOKING TIME: *20 minutes*
MAKES *3 cups*

185 g butter, chopped
¾ cup sugar
3 egg yolks, beaten
½ cup lemon juice
2 medium bananas, mashed
2 large passionfruit

1   Combine butter, sugar, egg yolks and lemon juice in heatproof bowl.

2   Stir over simmering water until butter is melted and mixture is smooth. Stir in bananas and passionfruit pulp.

3   Stir over simmering water until mixture is thickened and coats the back of a wooden spoon.

4   Pour into warm, sterilised jars and seal. When cold, label and date. Store in refrigerator until required.

Guava Jelly

Use slightly under-ripe guavas for best results.

PREPARATION TIME: *30 minutes*
plus overnight standing time
COOKING TIME: *45 minutes*
MAKES *3½ cups*

1 kg slightly under-ripe guavas
1 green apple
½ cup lemon juice
1 litre water
sugar

1   Cut guavas and apple into thick slices.

2   Combine guavas, apple, lemon juice and water in large saucepan or boiler. Bring to the boil and boil slowly, uncovered for 10 minutes. Break up guavas and apple with a wooden spoon and boil slowly for a further 10 minutes.

3   Strain mixture through muslin suspended over a bowl and stand overnight. Measure strained juice and return to saucepan. Add 1 cup of warmed sugar for each cup of juice and stir over heat until sugar is dissolved. Bring to the boil and boil rapidly until setting point is reached.

4   Remove from heat and pour into warm, sterilised jars. Label and date.

Sage Jelly

Brush roast loin of pork with 1 cup Sage Jelly 20 minutes before the end of cooking time. Use pan juices for sauce simply by boiling on top of stove and thickening with cornflour. When making individual pots of pâté, warm jelly until runny and pour into pots, setting a sage leaf in each.

PREPARATION TIME: *35 minutes*
plus 3 hours standing
COOKING TIME: *1¾ hours*
MAKES *2 litres*

8 medium green apples
2 medium red apples
40 fresh sage leaves
2 teaspoons grated lemon rind
⅔ cup lemon juice
sugar

1   Wash and dry fruit. Finely chop fruit and coarsely chop sage leaves.

2   Combine fruit including cores and seeds, leaves and rind in a large saucepan or boiler. Cover with water, bring to boil and simmer, covered, for 1 hour or until fruit is soft and pulpy.

3   Strain fruit through muslin bag suspended over a bowl for 3 hours. Measure juice and return to saucepan. Add lemon juice and heat until boiling. Add ¾ cup sugar per cup of juice. Return to the boil, stirring until sugar dissolves. Boil rapidly for 45 minutes or until setting point.

4   Remove jelly from the heat and stand 5 minutes. Pour into warm, sterilised jars. Allow to cool completely. (When almost set, sage leaves may be suspended in the jelly using a clean bamboo skewer). Seal jars. When cool, label and date.

After washing fruit or vegetable, ensure it is patted dry. The excess water can alter the proportions of the recipe.

Fruit butters can be stored for up to 6 months. They are best kept at least 3 weeks prior to using.

Rosemary, Tomato and Apple Jelly

This jelly makes an excellent and unusual glaze for carrots. Boil, steam or microwave 4 carrots (chopped); drain. Warm ½ cup jelly and pour over carrots. Serve glazed carrots as an accompaniment to a roast dinner.

PREPARATION TIME: *25 minutes*
COOKING TIME: *1¾ hours*
MAKES *1.75 litres*

7 medium green apples
2 medium pears
1 ripe tomato
1 cup fresh rosemary leaves
⅔ cup lemon juice
sugar

1 Wash apples, pears and tomato; drain. Finely chop apples, pears and tomato; coarsely chop rosemary.

2 Combine fruit (including cores and seeds), tomato and rosemary in a large saucepan or boiler and cover with water. Bring to the boil and simmer covered for about 1 hour or until fruit is soft and pulpy.

3 Strain fruit mixture through muslin bag suspended over a bowl. Measure juice and return to saucepan with lemon juice. Heat until boiling. Add ¾ cup sugar per cup of juice. Return to the boil, stirring until sugar dissolves. Boil rapidly, uncovered for ¾ hour or until setting point is reached.

4 Remove cooked jelly from the heat and stand 5 minutes. Pour into warm, sterilised jars and cool before sealing. When almost set, a sprig of fresh rosemary may be suspended in the jelly, using a clean bamboo skewer. When cool, label and date.

Apple Passionfruit Jam

PREPARATION TIME: *40 minutes*
COOKING TIME: *1½ hours*
MAKES *1.75 litres*

1.5 kg apples
2 cups water
1 teaspoon lemon rind
1 teaspoon lime rind
¼ cup lime juice
¼ cup lemon juice
5½ cups sugar, warmed
1¼ cups passionfruit pulp (about 16 passionfruit)

1 Wash, peel, remove seeds and finely chop apples.

2 Combine apples, water and rinds in a large saucepan or boiler. Bring to the boil and simmer, covered 30 minutes, or until apples are soft.

3 Add juices and boil uncovered for 10 minutes. Add the warm sugar and stir until dissolved. Stir in pulp. Boil rapidly, uncovered, for about 50 minutes or until setting point is reached.

4 Remove cooked jam from heat and stand 10 minutes. Pour into warm, sterilised jars and seal immediately. When cool, label and date.

Choko Passionfruit Jam and golden croissants — perfect partners to enjoy on a sunny morning

AUTUMN PICKLES

Sweet and Sour Pears
49

Sweet Mustard Pickle
49

Antipasto Pickle
50

Pickled Cauliflower
50

Pickled Dried Figs
50

Vegetable Relish
52

Oriental Mixed Pickles
52

Spiced Beans
52

Savoury Fruit Sauce
53

Sweet and Sour Pears

Choose firm pears for this recipe. If pears are not ripe you may need to increase sugar slightly. Place a pear half on serving plate with fresh figs or dates, plus slices of fresh Parmesan cheese. Serve as a summer entrée or with salad for a light luncheon.

PREPARATION TIME: *15 minutes*
COOKING TIME: *10–12 minutes*
MAKES *500 g*

3 firm pears, peeled, halved and cored
1 lemon, juice and strips of rind
½ cup sugar
1 cup white vinegar
1 cinnamon stick
1 teaspoon whole cloves

1   Place pears in saucepan with lemon juice and rind and cover with cold water. Heat until simmering. Cook until pears are just tender when tested with a skewer.

2   Meanwhile slowly heat sugar, vinegar and spices, stirring until sugar dissolves. Heat until boiling then remove from heat.

3   Carefully pack pears tightly into jars with cinnamon and cloves. Pour hot liquid over pears to cover completely. Cover at once with airtight lids. When cool, label and date. Mature 2 weeks before opening; store up to 4 months.

Sweet Mustard Pickle

Two teaspoons of finely chopped fresh chilli may be added in step 3 for a spicy mustard pickle. Stir half a cup of Sweet Mustard Pickle into a hot beef curry, just before serving.

PREPARATION TIME: *30 minutes plus*
overnight standing
COOKING TIME: *15 minutes*
MAKES *1.5 litres*

1 kg tomatoes
2 onions
2 small cucumbers
1 red capsicum
1 pear
2.5 litres water

½ cup salt
2 cups sugar
1½ cups malt vinegar
2 tablespoons plain flour
2 teaspoons dry mustard
1 teaspoon curry powder
¼ teaspoon cayenne pepper
2 teaspoons turmeric
¼ cup malt vinegar, extra

1   Peel and slice tomatoes and onions. Slice unpeeled cucumbers and capsicum. Finely chop pear. Place vegetables in a large bowl and cover with water. Sprinkle with salt and stand overnight.

2   Put ingredients in bowl into a large saucepan or boiler. Bring slowly to boil and simmer 10 minutes or until vegetables are soft. Strain off liquid.

3   Add sugar and vinegar to pan with vegetables, bring slowly to boil and simmer 3 minutes, stirring until sugar is dissolved. Blend flour, mustard, curry, cayenne, turmeric and vinegar until smooth. Add to pan, bring to boil and simmer until mixture is thick, stirring constantly.

4   Remove from heat. Spoon into warm, sterilised jars and seal. When cool, label and date. Store 10 days before opening to mellow flavours.

Whole spices are best used for pickling as they leave no sediment. Try cinnamon sticks, cloves, star anise or mustard seeds.

Sweet and Sour Pears

Antipasto Pickle

Fresh herbs, chopped chilli and garlic slivers may be added to this pickle.

PREPARATION TIME: *30 minutes*
COOKING TIME: *15 minutes*
MAKES *about 1.5 litres*

¼ medium cauliflower
2 medium carrots
2 sticks celery
1 cup white vinegar
1 cup Italian salad dressing
1¼ cups water
1 teaspoon salt
¼ teaspoon cayenne pepper
1 tablespoon chopped fresh oregano
16 stuffed green olives

1   Cut cauliflower into small florets. Cut carrots and celery into diagonal slices.

2   Combine vinegar, dressing, water, salt and cayenne pepper in large saucepan or boiler. Bring to the boil. Add vegetables and simmer, covered, 5 minutes.

3   Add oregano and olives; remove from heat.

4   Pack vegetables into warm, sterilised jars and cover with hot vinegar mixture. Cool, then seal, label and date.

Pickled Cauliflower

Serve cauliflower with warm steamed broccoli and carrots. Drizzle with olive oil and serve as winter salad.

PREPARATION TIME: *10 minutes*
plus overnight standing
COOKING TIME: *15 minutes*
MAKES *2 litres*

½ cup salt
1.25 litres water
1 large cauliflower
5 cups cider vinegar
2 tablespoons sugar
1 teaspoon whole cloves
1 teaspoon whole allspice
1 teaspoon peppercorns

2 cinnamon sticks
5 dried red chillies
6 radishes

1   Combine salt and water in saucepan and stir over low heat until dissolved. Chop cauliflower coarsely. Place cauliflower in large bowl and cover with salted water. Cover with dry cloth and stand overnight. Drain.

2   Place vinegar, sugar, cloves, allspice, peppercorns, cinnamon and chillies into saucepan. Bring slowly to boil and simmer covered, 15 minutes.

3   Combine cauliflower with chopped radishes. Pack into warm, sterilised jars and add whole cloves, allspice, peppercorns, cinnamon and chillies. Return pickling mixture to heat and bring to the boil. Pour boiling liquid over vegetables and seal. When cool, label and date.

Pickled Dried Figs

These delicious Pickled Figs can be drained, chopped and added to seasonings for roast pork or roast lamb.

PREPARATION TIME: *15 minutes*
COOKING TIME: *30 minutes*
MAKES *1 litre*

500 g dried figs
1 cup cider vinegar
½ cup brown sugar
1 tablespoon golden syrup
1 cinnamon stick
4 whole allspice
4 whole cloves
6 peppercorns
¼ teaspoon salt

1   Place figs in saucepan and cover with water. Bring to the boil. Cover and simmer for 15 minutes. Drain figs and return to saucepan.

2   Add remaining ingredients to pan and bring to the boil. Cover; simmer a further 15 minutes, stirring occasionally.

3   Remove from heat and pack figs into warm, sterilised jars. Pour cooking liquid over figs to cover and seal. When cold, label and date.

Antipasto is a delicious Italian hors d'oeuvre where a combination of cold meats, cheeses, fruits and pickled vegetables are served to whet the appetite before the main meal.

Pickled Cauliflower in sauceboat and Antipasto Pickle on plate

Vegetable Relish

Any seasonal vegetable may be used in this relish.

PREPARATION TIME: *20 minutes*
COOKING TIME: *20 minutes*
MAKES *2 litres*

½ cabbage
2 zucchini
2 onions
1 carrot
1 green capsicum
3 cups cider vinegar
1 cup water
½ cup sugar
2 teaspoons salt
3 bay leaves
2 teaspoons prepared horseradish
1 teaspoon peppercorns

1   Thinly slice cabbage. Coarsely chop zucchini and onions. Slice carrot and capsicum into thin strips.

2   Place all ingredients except cabbage in large saucepan or boiler. Bring slowly to boil and simmer for 10 minutes. Add cabbage to pan and simmer a further 10 minutes or until mixture is thick.

3   Remove from heat and spoon into warm, sterilised jars. Seal. When cool, label and date. Store 10 days before opening to mellow flavours.

For pickles and chutneys it is best to use coarse cooking salt. Table salt is unsuitable and will produce a cloudy brine.

Oriental Mixed Pickles

Stir-fry some beef in a wok and add sufficient Oriental Mixed Pickles for a serving. Thicken slightly with cornflour if required.

PREPARATION TIME: *40 minutes plus overnight standing*
COOKING TIME: *10 minutes*
MAKES *2 litres*

2 cucumbers
1 stick celery
½ small cauliflower
1 red capsicum
1 green apple
2 onions

2.5 litres boiling water
½ cup salt
1 cup sugar
2½ cups white vinegar
1 tablespoon chopped fresh ginger
3 whole star anise
1 tablespoon celery seed
5 small garlic cloves
2 tablespoons soy sauce

1   Coarsely chop cucumbers, celery, cauliflower and capsicum. Peel and grate apple and cut onions into wedges. Place vegetables in a large bowl. Combine salt with water, pour over vegetables in bowl, cover with dry cloth and stand overnight; drain vegetables.

2   Place sugar, vinegar, ginger, star anise, celery seed, garlic and soy sauce in large saucepan or boiler. Bring to boil, and simmer for 5 minutes. Add the vegetables to the pan, bring to boil and simmer 5 minutes.

3   Remove from heat. Pack vegetables into warm, sterilised jars. Return pickling mixture to heat and bring to the boil. Pour boiling liquid over vegetables and seal. When cool, label and date.

Spiced Beans

Combine 1 cup Spiced Beans and liquid with 3 cups of boiled cubed potatoes to make a wholesome family salad.

PREPARATION TIME: *30 minutes plus 2 hours standing*
COOKING TIME: *40 minutes*
MAKES *1.75 litres*

1 cup dried canellini beans
1 cup dried borlotti beans
½ cup sugar
1½ cups cider vinegar
5 bay leaves
4 cloves garlic, bruised
1 tablespoon peppercorns
1 tablespoon salt
1 tablespoon chopped fennel leaves
½ teaspoon cinnamon
4 whole red chillies

1   Soak beans in boiling water for 2 hours.

2   Place beans with water in large saucepan or boiler. Bring to boil and boil rapidly for about 30 minutes or until beans are tender. Drain, refresh under cold water, drain again.

3   Place sugar, vinegar, bay leaves, garlic, peppercorns, salt, fennel and cinnamon in a large saucepan or boiler. Bring to the boil and simmer, uncovered, 3 minutes. Add beans to pan and simmer a further 5 minutes.

4   Remove from heat. Pack beans into warm, sterilised jars, three-quarters full. Add whole chillies, peppercorns and bay leaves. Return pickling mixture to heat and bring to the boil. Pour boiling liquid over to cover beans, top with olive oil and seal. When cool, label and date. Store 10 days before opening.

Savoury Fruit Sauce

Savoury Fruit Sauce is an ideal sauce for steaks or lamb or pork chops. Try adding some to your favourite marinade for barbecued meats.

PREPARATION TIME: *30 minutes*
COOKING TIME: *30 minutes*
MAKES *1.5 litres*

3 green apples
1 onion
2 cloves garlic
250 g dates, chopped
400 g can tomatoes, chopped
¼ cup golden syrup
3 cups water
2 tablespoons sugar
½ cup white vinegar
2 teaspoons dry mustard
1 teaspoon ground chillies

1   Coarsely chop unpeeled apples, peeled onion and garlic.

2   Combine all ingredients in a large saucepan or boiler; bring to the boil. Cover and simmer for 30 minutes.

3   Process mixture in food processor in several batches until smooth. Rub through strainer.

4   Pour mixture into warm, sterilised bottles or jars and seal. When cold, label and date. Store in refrigerator until required.

When a recipe calls for apples, always use the best cooking apples in season at the time.

Spiced Beans

AUTUMN CHUTNEYS

Grape Sauce
55

Tomato Apple Chutney
55

Spiced Fruit Chutney
55

Banana Date Chutney
56

Fig Chutney
57

Apple, Tomato and Mint Chutney
57

Fruity Relish
57

Apple and Dried Fruit Chutney
58

Barbecue Sauce
58

Apple and Capsicum Chutney
58

Grape Sauce

Use white or black grapes for this recipe. If a thicker sauce is required add pulp back to step 3 after puréeing. Serve with roast pork, chicken, veal, curries, meatballs and other meat dishes.

PREPARATION TIME: *15 minutes*
COOKING TIME: *40–60 minutes*
MAKES *1 litre*

2 kg grapes, washed
2 cups vinegar
2 cups brown sugar
1 teaspoon ground ginger
½ teaspoon ground cloves
6 peppercorns
¼ teaspoon chilli powder
2 cloves garlic

1   Place grapes and vinegar in a large saucepan or boiler and squash grapes with a wooden spoon.

2   Simmer gently 20 minutes or until grape skins are tender. Strain and push grapes through a coarse sieve.

3   Return to saucepan and add remaining ingredients. Stir until boiling and simmer another 20–30 minutes.

4   Remove from heat and strain again. Pour into warm, sterilised jars and seal. When cool, label and date.

Tomato Apple Chutney

To peel tomatoes, place in a bowl, cover with boiling water for 1–2 minutes. Drain. Skin should peel away easily. Add 3 tablespoons of Tomato Apple Chutney to your favourite curry.

PREPARATION TIME: *30 minutes*
COOKING TIME: *2 hours*
MAKES *1.5 litres*

1 kg ripe firm tomatoes, peeled
6 large green apples
3 medium onions, diced
2 cups sugar
2 teaspoons salt
1 tablespoon curry powder

1 tablespoon dry mustard
3¾ cups cider vinegar
¾ cup sultanas
¾ cup raisins

1   Roughly chop tomatoes, peel, core and dice apples. Place tomatoes, apples and onions in large saucepan or boiler. Stir in sugar, salt, curry powder and mustard. Add vinegar.

2   Cook over low heat stirring until sugar has dissolved, then simmer for 10 minutes. Add sultanas and raisins and simmer for another 1 hour 45 minutes or until thick. Pour into warm, sterilised jars and seal. When cool, label and date.

Spiced Fruit Chutney

Any dried fruits may be used for this recipe. Use as a filling for festive mince tarts.

PREPARATION TIME: *20 minutes*
COOKING TIME: *45 minutes*
MAKES *about 2 litres*

2 cups dried apricots
1 cup dried pears
1 cup raisins
2 teaspoons grated fresh ginger
2 tablespoons cider vinegar
1 teaspoon allspice
1 teaspoon ground cardamom
3 cups apple juice
2 large green apples, unpeeled, cored and sliced thinly

1   Coarsely chop apricots and pears.

2   Place apricots, pears, raisins, ginger, vinegar and spices in a large heavy based saucepan or boiler. Add half the apple juice and mix well. Heat until boiling, reduce heat and cover. Simmer for 20 minutes, stirring occasionally. Add apples and remaining apple juice. Cover and simmer until the apples are tender, about 10 minutes, stirring occasionally.

3   Ladle into warm, sterilised jars and seal. Label and date when cool.

Dried fruits give richness, colour and sweetness to chutneys. Choose good quality dried fruits, rinse them well and dry with absorbent paper before adding to chutney mixtures.

A selection of beautifully presented chutneys can make an ideal gift for Christmas and birthdays.

Banana Date Chutney

Fruits low in pectin content — bananas, cherries (sweet or ripe), elderberries, figs, grapes, marrow, melons, peaches, pears, rhubarb, strawberries.

This chutney is best if kept in the refrigerator. It makes an excitingly different accompaniment to spicy curries and other oriental dishes.

Left: Apple, Tomato and Mint Chutney
Right: Banana Date Chutney served with rice and fresh figs

PREPARATION TIME: *45 minutes*
COOKING TIME: *45 minutes*
MAKES *2 litres*

1 kg bananas
500 g onions
375 g pitted dates
2 cloves garlic, crushed
1½ cups malt vinegar
1½ cups sultanas
⅔ cup drained preserved ginger, chopped
1 cup orange juice
½ cup lemon juice
1 tablespoon yellow mustard seeds
5 whole cloves
1 teaspoon salt
¼ teaspoon hot chilli flakes

1   Peel and mash bananas; chop onions and dates coarsely.

2   In a large, heavy saucepan or boiler combine the bananas, onions, dates, garlic and vinegar. Mix well and heat until boiling. Reduce heat, cover and simmer for 20 minutes. Add sultanas, ginger, orange and lemon juice, mustard seeds, cloves, salt and chilli flakes. Heat until boiling. Reduce heat and simmer, stirring frequently until thickened, 15–20 minutes more.

3   Ladle into warm, sterilised jars and seal. When cool, label and date.

Fig Chutney

This dark tasty chutney can be served with leg ham or roast pork.

PREPARATION TIME: *20 minutes plus overnight standing*
COOKING TIME: *2 hours*
MAKES *1.5 litres*

500 g dried figs
5 onions
250 g raisins
2 cloves garlic, crushed
4 cups sugar
2 cups malt vinegar
2 cups white vinegar
2 teaspoons salt
½ teaspoon ground cinnamon
¼ cup lime juice
¼ cup pine nuts

1   Cover figs in boiling water overnight; drain. Halve figs. Finely chop onions and coarsely chop raisins.

2   Place all ingredients, except nuts, in a large saucepan or boiler. Bring slowly to boil and simmer uncovered for about 2 hours or until mixture is thick, stirring occasionally.

3   Remove cooked chutney from the heat and stand 5 minutes; stir in pine nuts. Spoon into warm, sterilised jars and seal immediately. When cool, label and date.

Apple, Tomato and Mint Chutney

Serve chutney with cold sliced meats. Half cup of chutney combined with plain yoghurt can be used as an accompaniment to curries.

PREPARATION TIME: *1 hour*
COOKING TIME: *2½ hours*
MAKES *1.5 litres*

1 kg green apples
1 kg tomatoes
3 onions
⅔ cup mint leaves
½ cup parsley
1 cup raisins
½ cup orange juice
⅓ cup lemon juice
3 cups brown sugar
2 teaspoons salt
2 cups cider vinegar

1   Wash, peel and finely chop apples, tomatoes and onions. Finely chop fresh herbs.

2   Place all ingredients in a large saucepan or boiler. Bring slowly to boil and simmer for about 2½ hours or until mixture is thick, stirring occasionally.

3   Remove cooked chutney from the heat and stand 5 minutes. Spoon into warm, sterilised jars and seal immediately. When cool, label and date.

Chutney, sauces and pickles were introduced to England from China and India in the seventeenth century. These spicy condiments handed down from the British Raj, were welcome additions to British meals.

Fruity Relish

If you prefer a less sharp flavour, slightly reduce the amount of vinegar used. Store relish in refrigerator. This relish is best made in small quantities. Fruity Relish is a delightful accompaniment for barbecued or roast lamb, beef, turkey and pork. Add a tablespoon or two to your favourite meatloaf or meatball recipe.

PREPARATION TIME: *10 minutes*
COOKING TIME: *1½ hours*
MAKES *1 cup*

425 g can fruit salad in natural juice
1 large white onion, finely chopped
½ cup packed brown sugar
¼ cup malt vinegar
½ teaspoon ground ginger
½ teaspoon ground cinnamon
¼ teaspoon ground allspice
¼ teaspoon cayenne pepper
2 teaspoons chopped fresh mint

1   In a large saucepan or boiler, (not aluminium) combine undrained fruit salad, onion, sugar, vinegar, ginger, cinnamon, allspice and cayenne pepper.

2   Heat to boiling, then reduce heat, stirring occasionally. Simmer gently for 45 minutes to 1 hour. Add the mint. Simmer until thickened and well flavoured, about 15–20 minutes.

3   Spoon into warm, sterilised jars and seal. When cool, label and date.

Apple and Dried Fruit Chutney

Combine ¼ cup Apple and Dried Fruit Chutney with ½ cup cottage cheese. Serve with fresh vegetable sticks.

PREPARATION TIME: *30 minutes*
COOKING TIME: *1 hour
10 minutes*
MAKES 2.5 litres

*5 medium green apples
2 onions
250 g dates
1 cup dried apricots
200 g packet dried pears
1 cup raisins
1 cup sultanas
1 cup brown sugar
½ teaspoon cayenne pepper
3 cups malt vinegar*

1 Wash, peel and remove seeds from apples. Finely chop apples, onions, dates, apricots and pears.

2 Place apples, onions, dates, apricots, pears, raisins and sultanas in a large saucepan or boiler. Add sugar, pepper and vinegar to pan. Bring slowly to boil and simmer uncovered for about 60 minutes or until mixture is thick, stirring occasionally.

3 Remove cooked chutney from the heat and stand 5 minutes. Pour into warm, sterilised jars and seal immediately. When cool, label and date.

> To reduce the cooking and preparation times of chutneys, mince the ingredients in a food processor or blender prior to cooking.

Barbecue Sauce

Use as a baste for steak and chops or add to marinades for meat or chicken. Add to mayonnaise to make a tangy cocktail sauce.

PREPARATION TIME: *10 minutes*
COOKING TIME: *20 minutes*
MAKES 2½ cups

*2 tablespoons oil
1 onion, finely chopped
1 clove garlic, crushed
½ cup tomato sauce*

*¼ cup fruit chutney
1 cup peach or apricot nectar
¼ cup cider vinegar
2 tablespoons brown sugar
1 tablespoon Worcestershire sauce
½ cup water*

1 Heat oil in saucepan. Add onion and garlic and stir over heat until onion is soft.

2 Add remaining ingredients to pan, bring to the boil, and simmer for 15 minutes, stirring occasionally

3 Strain sauce through sieve. Pour sauce into warm, sterilised bottles or jars and seal. When cold, label and date. Store in refrigerator until required.

Apple and Capsicum Chutney

Add 1 cup of Apple and Capsicum Chutney to fresh breadcrumbs and use as a stuffing for loin of pork, roast turkey or roast chicken.

PREPARATION TIME: *1 hour*
COOKING TIME: *2 hours*
MAKES *about 2 litres*

*2 kg green apples
500 g red capsicums
750 g onions
250 g raisins
¾ cup sultanas
2½ cups malt vinegar
500 g brown sugar
1 tablespoon salt
1 tablespoon treacle
2 teaspoons cayenne pepper*

1 Peel, core and chop apples into small pieces, cut capsicum into small squares and slice the onions.

2 Put apples, capsicum, onions, raisins, sultanas and vinegar into a large saucepan or boiler. Add the sugar, salt, treacle and cayenne pepper and heat gently, stirring until sugar has dissolved. Bring to boiling point, reduce heat and simmer, stirring occasionally, about 2 hours.

3 Ladle into warm, sterilised jars and seal airtight. Label and date when cool.

Apple and Capsicum Chutney

JELLY MAKING

Jellies are made on the same principle as jams but the fruit is strained so that a clear, full flavoured jelly results. While the basic method is the same as jam making, the whole process is more time-consuming and requires more attention to obtain a good clear jelly with a characteristic colour. The jelly should set, but shouldn't be rubbery or thin in consistency.

The amount of jelly resulting will be significantly less than for jam made with the same amount of fruit. This is not a disadvantage, however, if you have an abundance of home grown produce in season.

EQUIPMENT

The equipment needed to make jellies is the same as required for jam making with the addition of a jelly bag for straining the juice. Specially made bags can be purchased; however, a double layer of muslin or a clean, boiled cotton or linen cloth will suffice. The fabric or jelly bag needs to be suspended above a bowl where it cannot come into direct contact with the filtered liquid. This can be done by tying the cloth to the four legs of an upturned chair or stool with the catchment bowl underneath.

STEPS IN MAKING JELLY

Preparing the fruit Prepare under-ripe fruit as for jam; however, stalks, cores and skins may be included since the fruit will not be present in the final product. Fruit should be cut fairly small to allow for the maximum amount of pectin to be released during cooking.

2 Place fruit in a large saucepan or boiler, cover with water, and simmer until fruit is soft and pulpy.

Softening the fruit The fruit is cooked in a preserving pan or large saucepan to soften the fruit and extract both flavour and pectin. Slow cooking is essential at this stage to gain a full flavoured juice with good setting qualities. After cooking the fruit the mixture should be tested for its pectin content. If it is low in pectin, continue cooking for a further 10–15 minutes and test again. It is possible if using fruits low in pectin or over-ripe fruit that a little commercial pectin will need to be added to the fruit to give a good gel.

1 Wash fruit and finely chop, using cores, seeds, stems and skins.

3 Suspend muslin cloth between the legs of an upturned stool. Place bowl underneath and strain fruit and liquid.

Straining the pulp This step is essentially what makes the difference between jam and jelly. The pulp and juice are spooned or poured into a jelly bag and allowed to drip into a bowl underneath. It is important that the bag doesn't come in contact with the strained liquid, nor should the bag be squeezed to extract the liquid since this will result in a milky gel. The process generally takes a few hours but this will vary depending on the fruit, the type of fabric in the jelly bag and the quantity made. After the liquid has strained, continue with the cooking as soon as possible. If left the mixture can begin to ferment, giving the jelly a tainted, unpleasant flavour.

Adding the sugar The amount of sugar needed will depend on the yield of the juice. As a general rule allow equal quantities by volume of juice to sugar; however, this may vary depending on the fruit used. The recipe will be the guide.

5   Test setting point by placing a little jelly on a cold saucer. When cold, push jelly slightly — it should wrinkle.

Testing for Setting Test jelly the same way as testing jam.

Bottling Before bottling remove scum from surface of the jelly by skimming with a metal spoon. Pour jelly into sterilised jars.

6   Remove any scum from the surface of the jelly with a metal spoon. Pour into sterilised jars.

4   Place measured juice in a saucepan. Bring to the boil and add sugar, stirring until sugar dissolves.

FRUIT BUTTERS AND CURDS

Fruit butter and fruit curds are often mistaken for the same type of preserve. While this is not the case, they are generally grouped together due to their similiar consistencies. Fruit butters are made largely from a fruit purée and sugar and cooked until a paste-like consistency results.

STEPS IN MAKING FRUIT BUTTER

Preparing the Fruit As for jams and jellies, remove any blemished or spoilt parts of the fruit.

Softening the Fruit Place fruit in pan with cold water and cook slowly until fruit becomes soft and sufficiently mushy to form a purée.

Puréeing Fruit Some fruits will cook down to a purée while others will need to be placed in a food processor or blender to purée. If neither of these is available the mixture can be pushed through a sieve with the back of a wooden spoon.

Adding the Sugar The sugar is added and dissolved before returning to the boil. The mixture is then simmered until it is thick.

To Test Place a little mixture on a saucer; when ready the mixture should not have any liquid weeping from it.

Bottling Spoon into warm, sterilised jars and seal while hot.

1 Prepare fruit by washing and removing any stems and bruised or blemished parts.

2 Place fruit and liquid in a large saucepan or boiler, and simmer until fruit softens.

3 Push fruit through a fine sieve with a wooden spoon until smooth.

4 Return fruit purée to saucepan. Stir in sugar over low heat until sugar dissolves.

5 To test for setting point, place a little mixture on a cold saucer. Mixture should be firm without liquid weeping.

6 Spoon into warm sterilised jars and seal. Label and date when cool.

FRUIT CURDS

Fruit curds are sometimes referred to as 'butters' in the case of lemon butter, hence the confusion. A fruit curd is made with fruit purées or juices, sugar, eggs and butter and sometimes flavoured with spices and rinds of the fruit.

The keeping qualities of fruit curds are restricted by the mere nature of the ingredients. Normally a fridge life of up to 3 months is the maximum storage time recommended. The base of most curds is either a mixture of citrus juice and rind or a concentrated fruit purée.

STEPS IN MAKING FRUIT CURDS

The First Stage Combine the fruit base, sugar and butter in a heatproof bowl. The bowl is placed over a saucepan of simmering water and stirred occasionally until the sugar and butter dissolve.

Adding the Eggs This is the next step and it is important the whole eggs or often egg yolks are beaten very well prior to adding to the base mixture. If a little warm base mixture is added to the beaten eggs prior to adding to mixture, there is less likelihood of the eggs cooling immediately on adding.

Cooking the Mixture This is continued over simmering water, stirring constantly until the mixture thickens. When mixture forms a custard-like coating on the back of a metal spoon, remove from the heat.

Bottling Spoon into warm, sterilised jars and seal while hot. It is important jars are not too hot when adding the mixture, otherwise it will curdle.

1 *Push fruit purée through a fine sieve with a wooden spoon until smooth.*

2 *Place fruit purée, sugar and butter in a heatproof bowl over simmering water. Stir to dissolve butter and sugar.*

3 *Add a little fruit mixture to the beaten eggs and mix well. Whisk egg mixture into fruit base.*

4 *Over simmering water, stir mixture until it thickens.*

5 *Fruit curd is ready when mixture forms a coating over the back of a metal spoon.*

6 *Pour fruit curd immediately into warm sterilised jars.*

Winter

Winter's bounty includes zesty, juicy citrus fruits such as orange, lemon, grapefruit and lime that lend themselves well to glistening marmalades and jams. Earthy winter vegetables like cabbage, beetroot and cauliflower combine with spices and vinegars to produce full flavoured pickles and chutneys. Tempt and captivate your taste buds with Lime Curry Pickles, pungent Spiced Mushrooms or Kiwi Lime Jam.

Orange Marmalade is used to glaze a steamed pudding, ideal for winter nights

WINTER JAMS

Kiwi Lime Jam
67

Apple Kiwi Jam
67

Ginger Apple Marmalade
67

Three Fruit Marmalade
68

Grapefruit Marmalade
68

Golden Marmalade
68

Fruity Pumpkin Conserve
70

Quince Conserve
70

Chunky Orange Marmalade
70

Orange Marmalade
72

Lemon Butter
73

Lemon Marmalade
73

Apricot and Lemon Jam
73

Kiwi Lime Jam

This is a bitter-sweet jam. If a sweeter jam is required reduce limes to 250 g and increase kiwi fruit by 250 g. Use Kiwi Lime Jam as a tangy glaze for a steamed pudding.

PREPARATION TIME: *35 minutes plus overnight standing.*
COOKING TIME: *60 minutes*
MAKES *1.5 litres*

500 g ripe limes
2 cups water
1 kg kiwi fruit
5 cups sugar, warmed

1   Wash and thinly slice the limes and cover with the water. Leave to stand overnight. Next day peel kiwi fruit and chop coarsely.

2   Put limes and water into a large heavy based saucepan or boiler. Cover and simmer gently until peel has softened, about 20–30 minutes. Add chopped kiwi fruit, cover, and simmer another 10 minutes. Remove lid.

3   Add warmed sugar and stir until sugar dissolves. Increase heat, stir frequently and simmer until setting point is reached.

4   Remove from heat and stand about 3 minutes. Pour into warm, sterilised jars and seal. When cool, label and date.

Apple Kiwi Jam

Use Apple Kiwi Jam in the centre of home-made jam doughnuts or in the base of coconut tartlets.

PREPARATION TIME: *20 minutes*
COOKING TIME: *1 hour 10 minutes*
MAKES *2 litres*

1.5 kg kiwi fruit
4 green apples
½ cup water
½ cup lemon juice
5 cups sugar, warmed

1   Peel and coarsely chop kiwi fruit and apples.

2   Combine kiwi fruit, apples and water in a large saucepan. Bring to the boil and simmer, uncovered, for about 30 minutes or until fruit is soft. Stir in juice.

3   Add the warm sugar and stir until dissolved. Boil rapidly, uncovered, for about 40 minutes until setting point is reached.

4   Remove cooked jam from the heat and stand 5 minutes. Pour into warm, sterilised jars and seal immediately. When cool, label and date.

Ginger Apple Marmalade

For a special occasion afternoon tea, sandwich together a ginger sponge which has been spread with Ginger Apple Marmalade and cream; dust top layer with icing sugar.

PREPARATION TIME: *30 minutes*
COOKING TIME: *45 minutes*
MAKES *5 cups*

1 kg cooking apples
4 cups sugar, warmed
1 cup water
2 tablespoons grated fresh ginger
grated rind and juice of 2 large lemons

1   Peel, core and chop the apples finely.

2   Put sugar and water into large saucepan or boiler and bring to boiling point, stirring until the sugar has dissolved. Add the ginger, lemon rind, juice and apples. Reduce heat and simmer, stirring occasionally, until setting point is reached.

3   Spoon into warm, sterilised jars and seal immediately. When cool, label and date.

Partially freeze citrus fruit prior to slicing for marmalades. This firms the fruit making cutting easier.

Seville oranges originated from the Himalayas and were brought west from India by the Arabs to Spain. These bitter tasting fruits are unsuitable for eating raw. They are mainly used for making marmalades, orange-flower water and orange-flavoured liqueurs.

Three Fruit Marmalade

This tangy Fruit Marmalade is a favourite topping for breakfast toast, muffins and croissants. It can also be used in an interesting dipping sauce. Combine ⅓ cup of marmalade with ⅓ cup soy sauce and serve with your favourite party meatballs or spring rolls.

PREPARATION TIME: *25 minutes plus overnight soaking*
COOKING TIME: *30 minutes*
MAKES *1.5 litres*

1 grapefruit
1 orange, sliced
2 lemons, sliced
7 cups water
6 cups sugar

1   Peel grapefruit, discard rind and cut pith into small pieces. Cut grapefruit into quarters and remove seeds and core. Place pith, seeds and core in a square of muslin tied with string.

2   Cut grapefruit quarters into thin slices and put into large bowl. Add orange and lemon slices and the water, cover with a plate to keep fruit down in water and leave overnight.

3   Next day, transfer to a heavy based saucepan or boiler with muslin bag and cook gently until fruit is soft and liquid is reduced by half. Remove muslin bag and squeeze out as much liquid as possible. Add the sugar, stir until dissolved and bring to boiling point.

4   Boil rapidly until setting point is reached. Remove from heat, leave for 10 minutes and then stir gently. Ladle into sterilised jars and seal airtight. When cool, label and date.

Golden Marmalade

Serve Golden Marmalade with warm muffins or scones.

PREPARATION TIME: *10 minutes plus overnight soaking*
COOKING TIME: *45 minutes–1 hour*
MAKES *3 cups*

1 medium carrot
1 medium lemon
1 large orange
3¾ cups boiling water
3 cups sugar, warmed

1   Peel and grate the carrot, cut the lemon and orange into quarters and slice thinly. Put into a bowl, pour the boiling water over, cover and stand overnight.

2   Next day bring to boiling point, then cook gently until the rinds are tender and the liquid is reduced by about half.

3   Add the warmed sugar and stir until sugar has dissolved. Boil rapidly until setting point is reached.

4   Remove from heat. Leave for 10 minutes, pour into warm, sterilised jars and seal. When cool, label and date.

Grapefruit Marmalade

Combine ½ cup of Grapefruit Marmalade and 2 tablespoons whisky. Use as a glaze for a leg or roll of veal. Brush glaze over veal during baking.

PREPARATION TIME: *35 minutes*
COOKING TIME: *1 hour 40 minutes*
MAKES *1 litre*

750 g grapefruit
2 medium lemons
2 litres water
6 cups sugar, warmed

1   Peel grapefruit and lemons thinly. Cut the peel into very fine strips and put into large saucepan or boiler. Remove pith from fruit and cut flesh into small pieces, reserving seeds.

2   Tie seeds and some pith in a piece of muslin and add to the peel with the water. Bring water to boiling point then simmer until peel is tender and liquid reduced by half.

3   Add sugar, stir until dissolved then boil rapidly until setting point is reached. Leave 10 minutes. Skim gently, turn into warm, sterilised jars and seal. When cool, label and date.

In medieval times, a preserve called *marmelade* was made from quince, honey, wine and spices. By the sixteenth century it was being prepared from fruits and berries with the addition of sugar, when it became known as jam (using whole fruit) and jelly (using strained juices).

Clockwise from left: Three Fruit Marmalade, Golden Marmalade with toast, and Grapefruit Marmalade in a jar

Fruity Pumpkin Conserve

Use butternut pumpkin to make a sweet, full flavoured and deeply coloured chutney. Serve as an accompaniment to curries or roast poultry, a topping for hot scones, a filling for crêpes or a topping for flapjacks.

PREPARATION TIME: *15 minutes*
COOKING TIME: *30 minutes*
MAKES *about 1 litre*

1 kg pumpkin
200 g dried apricots, coarsely chopped
1 cup sultanas
2¼ cups sugar
2 tablespoons chopped preserved ginger
1 tablespoon grated lemon rind
¼ cup lemon juice
2 tablespoons toasted pine nuts

1   Remove skin and seeds from pumpkin and chop coarsely. Boil, steam or microwave pumpkin until soft; drain.

2   Combine all ingredients except pine nuts in large saucepan or boiler; stir over low heat until sugar has dissolved. Bring to the boil and simmer for about 15 minutes or until thickened. Stir occasionally, breaking up pumpkin.

3   Remove from heat, stir in pine nuts.

4   Spoon into warm, sterilised jars and seal. When cool, label and date. Refrigerate conserve after opening.

> If using very sweet oranges in orange marmalade, add a little lemon juice to increase the acid level. This helps form a firmer result.

> Trim thick skinned citrus fruit of any excess pith prior to cooking. (It is essential to leave *some* present since high quantities of pectin are present in the pith).

Quince Conserve

Blend or process ¼ cup Quince Conserve into your favourite salad dressing or vinaigrette.

PREPARATION TIME: *30 minutes*
COOKING TIME: *1½ hours*
MAKES *1.5 litres*

1.5 kg quinces
10 cups water
2 teaspoons grated lemon rind
¾ cup lemon juice
5½ cups sugar, warmed

1   Peel and core quinces and slice flesh thinly. Place peel and cores in muslin and tie.

2   Combine quinces, muslin bag, water and rind in a large saucepan or boiler. Bring to the boil and simmer, covered, for about 50 minutes or until fruit is pulpy. Discard muslin bag. Stir in juice.

3   Add the warm sugar and stir until dissolved. Boil rapidly uncovered, for about 40 minutes or until setting point is reached.

4   Remove cooked conserve from the heat and stand 10 minutes. Pour into warm, sterilised jars and seal immediately. When cool, label and date.

Chunky Orange Marmalade

Navel oranges are best used for this marmalade. Use as a topping for scones or brioches or add 1–2 tablespoons to fruit cake mixture for moistness and flavour.

PREPARATION TIME: *1 hour*
COOKING TIME: *1 hour 40 minutes*
MAKES *about 2 litres*

3 medium oranges
1 lemon
3.75 litres water
2.25 kg sugar, warmed

1   Cut oranges into quarters, discard seeds and slice thinly. Halve lemon, discard seeds and slice thinly.

2   Combine oranges, lemon and water in large saucepan or boiler. Bring to the boil and simmer, uncovered, for about 1 hour or until peels are tender.

3   Add the warmed sugar and stir until dissolved. Boil rapidly, uncovered until setting point is reached.

4   Remove marmalade from heat and stand 10 minutes. Pour into warm, sterilised jars. Seal when cold. Label and date.

Fruity Pumpkin Conserve and Quince Conserve

Orange Marmalade

Soaking the prepared citrus fruit overnight in the cooking liquid, reduces the initial cooking time when making marmalades.

This marmalade can be used in sweet or savoury sauces. Heat ½ cup Orange Marmalade with 1 tablespoon butter and 2 tablespoons Grand Marnier in large pan, add 6 folded pancakes and serve as Crêpes Suzette.

Combine ½ cup Marmalade with ¼ cup brandy and add to pan 1 cup pan juices of roast duck. Boil on high until juices have thickened slightly. Serve over sliced roast duck.

PREPARATION TIME: *15 minutes*
COOKING TIME: *1 hour 25 minutes*
MAKES *1 litre*

2 oranges
1 lemon
1.25 litres water

Lemon Butter

1 kg sugar, warmed
¼ cup slivered almonds

1   Slice oranges and lemon thinly. Place fruit and water in a large bowl. Cover with dry cloth and stand overnight.

2   Put ingredients in bowl into a large saucepan or boiler. Bring to the boil and simmer uncovered for 45 minutes or until rinds are soft and liquid is reduced by about half.

3   Add the warm sugar and stir until dissolved. Boil rapidly uncovered for about 40 minutes or until setting point is reached.

4   Remove cooked marmalade from the heat and stand 5 minutes. Stir in almonds. Pour into warm, sterilised jars and seal immediately. When cool, label and date.

Lemon Butter

Lemon Butter is a sweet, zesty filling for sponge cakes or butterfly cakes. Stir lemon butter into warm custard to give a tangy lemon sauce for puddings. Use as a topping for ice-cream or substitute for jam in bread and butter custard.

PREPARATION TIME: *10 minutes*
COOKING TIME: *15 minutes*
MAKES *about 2 cups*

3 eggs, beaten
1 cup sugar
1 tablespoon grated lemon rind
½ cup lemon juice
60 g butter, chopped

1   Combine all ingredients in heatproof bowl. Whisk constantly over simmering water until mixture thickens and coats the back of a metal spoon.

2   Remove from heat and pour into warm, sterilised jars. When cool, label and date. Store in the refrigerator until required.

Lemon Marmalade

The best lemons are firm, evenly coloured and heavy for their size. Deep yellow colour indicates a less acidic lemon.
Blend ½ cup Lemon Marmalade with 1 cup water and 1 tablespoon chopped fresh herbs. Heat and serve with grilled chicken or fish.
For a quick dessert spread ½ cup Lemon Marmalade over prepared 20 cm flan case; top with meringue and bake in hot oven.

PREPARATION TIME: *10 minutes*
COOKING TIME: *1 hour 25 minutes*
MAKES *2½ cups*

3 large lemons
1.25 litres water
1 kg sugar, warmed
¼ cup currants

1   Slice lemons thinly. Place lemons and water in a large bowl. Cover with dry cloth and stand overnight.

2   Put ingredients in bowl into a large saucepan or boiler. Bring to the boil and simmer uncovered for about 45 minutes or until rinds are soft and liquid is reduced by about half.

3   Add the warm sugar and stir until dissolved. Boil rapidly, uncovered, for about 40 minutes or until setting point is reached.

4   Remove cooked marmalade from the heat and stand 5 minutes. Stir in currants. Pour into warm, sterilised jars and seal immediately. When cool, label and date.

Apricot and Lemon Jam

This jam is a luscious topping for hot buttered toast or muffins.

PREPARATION TIME: *15 minutes plus overnight soaking*
COOKING TIME: *1 hour*
MAKES *2.5 litres*

500 g dried apricots
5 lemons
1.25 litres water
1 kg sugar, warmed

1   Soak apricots in half the water for 24 hours. Boil lemons in remaining water until soft.

2   When lemons are cold, slice thinly, removing but not discarding pips.

3   Boil apricots in soaking water until tender, add sugar and sliced lemons, together with water in which they were boiled and the pips tied in a small muslin bag. Boil until jam gels. Discard the muslin bag.

4   Ladle into warm, sterilised jars and seal. When cool, label and date.

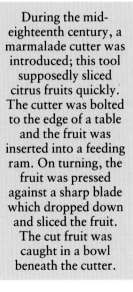

During the mid-eighteenth century, a marmalade cutter was introduced; this tool supposedly sliced citrus fruits quickly. The cutter was bolted to the edge of a table and the fruit was inserted into a feeding ram. On turning, the fruit was pressed against a sharp blade which dropped down and sliced the fruit. The cut fruit was caught in a bowl beneath the cutter.

WINTER PICKLES

Lime Curry Pickle
75

Spiced Mushrooms
75

Spiced Vinegar for Mushrooms
75

Beetroot Pickle
76

Caraway Cabbage Slaw
76

Vegetable Pickles
76

Beetroot and Cabbage Relish
77

Pickled Oranges
78

Pickled Lemons
78

Lime Curry Pickle

This zesty Lime Curry Pickle is a delicious accompaniment to curries. Steam or microwave chicken breasts, fan on plate and serve with warmed Lime Curry Pickle poured over the breast. Two tablespoons of Lime Curry liquid combined with 1 cup French dressing adds interest to many salads.

PREPARATION TIME: *30 minutes*
plus 3 days standing
COOKING TIME: *20 minutes*
MAKES *3 cups*

12 limes, washed
4 tablespoons salt
1½ cups good quality olive oil
1 tablespoon yellow mustard seeds,
toasted and crushed
2 teaspoons ground cumin
2 teaspoons ground ginger
½ teaspoon coarsely ground pepper
⅓ cup white wine vinegar
3 large cloves garlic, crushed
2 long red chillies, seeded and chopped
3 tablespoons sugar

1   Cut limes lengthwise into 8–10 wedges; cut wedges in half crosswise. In glass bowl, layer limes with the salt. Cover with clean cloth. Let stand in warm dry place for 3 days, stirring occasionally. Drain well.

2   In a large pan combine the oil, mustard seeds, cumin, ginger and pepper. Stir over a low heat until hot. Add limes with vinegar, garlic and chillies. Stir over a moderate heat for 5 minutes, then stir in sugar until dissolved. Add limes and simmer 1 minute.

3   Ladle into warm, sterilised jars and seal. When cool, label and date.

Spiced Mushrooms

Use small even-sized button mushrooms for this recipe. Spiced Mushrooms are best stored in the refrigerator. Serve with salads or with antipasto platter. For a tasty Asian inspired nibble, remove from liquid and roll in toasted sesame seeds. Chill and serve with pre-dinner drinks.

PREPARATION TIME: *15 minutes*
plus 24 hours standing
COOKING TIME: *10 minutes*
MAKES *about 1kg*

1 kg button mushrooms
¾ cup sugar
1 teaspoon sesame oil
4 tablespoons soy sauce
2 cups spiced vinegar
(see recipe below)
star anise (optional)

1   Wipe mushrooms clean, using a damp cloth. Cut stalk level with mushroom cap. Place in a large bowl.

2   In saucepan, stir sugar, sesame oil, soy sauce and spiced vinegar over low heat until sugar dissolves. Heat until the mixture boils.

3   Pour hot liquid over mushrooms. Cover and stand 24 hours.

4   Transfer mushrooms to jars with slotted spoon. Add star anise if desired. Pour soaking liquid into jars and cover with airtight lids. Label and date.

5   Mature 2 weeks in refrigerator before opening. Store up to 2 months.

Spiced Vinegar for Mushrooms

Use leftover vinegar as a base for your favourite French dressing.

PREPARATION TIME: *5 minutes*
COOKING TIME: *20 minutes*
MAKES *3 cups*

1 litre white wine vinegar
1 cinnamon stick
6 whole cloves
1 tablespoon coriander seeds
2 teaspoons yellow mustard seeds
1 teaspoon black peppercorns

1   Place all ingredients in saucepan without lid and heat until boiling. Reduce heat and simmer 15 minutes. Cool, then strain into sterilised jars. Seal, label and date.

Pickles can be stored for up to 2 years. They are best eaten in the first year for maximum crispness.

Soak wooden spoons in a mild bleach solution to remove strong odours after making pickles and chutneys.

Beetroot Pickle

Combine 1 cup of Beetroot Pickle with ½ cup sour cream and add to a potato salad for a tasty variation.

PREPARATION TIME: *20 minutes*
COOKING TIME: *1 hour*
MAKES *1 litre*

1 bunch of beetroot, (about 6, or 750 g peeled)
1 cup water
1 cup white vinegar
1 tablespoon dry mustard
1 cup white vinegar, extra
¾ cup firmly packed brown sugar
½ teaspoon ground allspice
½ teaspoon ground cloves
½ teaspoon cinnamon
1 teaspoon mustard seeds

1   Peel, halve, and thinly slice beetroot.

2   Put beetroot into a large saucepan with water and vinegar, and bring to the boil. Reduce heat, cover, and simmer until just tender.

3   Combine mustard, extra vinegar, sugar, allspice, cloves, cinnamon and mustard seeds, and add to the beetroot. Stir until boiling, reduce heat and simmer uncovered for 15 minutes.

4   Pack the beetroot into warm, sterilised jars, pour the liquid over and seal. When cool, label and date.

> The pickling of onions is one of the oldest forms of preserving, evidence of which has been found in the ruins of Pompeii. Today we enjoy pickled onions with cheese, tasty chutneys and crusty bread in the form of the traditional ploughman's lunch.

Caraway Cabbage Slaw

Red cabbage, savoy or Chinese cabbage may be used for this recipe. A colourful cold serving suggestion is to place a layer of slaw in salad bowl and top with layer of peeled sliced oranges. Repeat layers. Garnish with watercress. A tasty hot serving suggestion for our Caraway Cabbage Slaw is to place a layer of cooked sliced potato in casserole dish, top with layer of slaw then top with layer of potatoes. Sprinkle with grated Swiss cheese and 1 tablespoon caraway seeds. Bake in moderate oven until heated through and cheese is melted and browned.

PREPARATION TIME: *25 minutes plus overnight soaking*
COOKING TIME: *7 minutes*
MAKES *1 litre*

250 g red cabbage
1 large carrot, peeled
1 tablespoon salt
1 tablespoon caraway seeds
¼ cup sugar
1 cup white vinegar

1   By hand or food processor, finely shred cabbage and coarsely shred the carrot. Layer vegetables with salt in large bowl. Cover and stand 12 hours or overnight.

2   Rinse and dry vegetables thoroughly and mix in caraway seeds. Pack mixture into jars.

3   In saucepan, slowly heat sugar and vinegar, stirring until sugar dissolves. Heat until boiling and pour over slaw, then cover completely. Seal. When cool, label and date.

4   Mature 1 week before opening. Store up to 4 months.

Vegetable Pickles

For a zesty vegetable salad combine 1 cup drained Vegetable Pickles with three bean mix, chopped fresh herbs, olive oil and garlic.

PREPARATION TIME: *20 minutes plus overnight standing*
COOKING TIME: *15 minutes*
MAKES *2 litres*

½ small cauliflower
1 red capsicum
2 cucumbers
1 carrot
3 stalks celery
2 onions
½ cup salt
2.5 litres water
1.25 litres white vinegar
5 dried whole chillies
½ cup sugar
1 teaspoon celery seeds
1 tablespoon mustard seeds

1   Coarsely chop cauliflower, capsicum, cucumbers, carrot, celery and onions. Place vegetables in a large bowl, cover with water and sprinkle with salt. Cover with dry cloth and stand overnight. Drain, rinse and drain again.

2   Place vinegar, chillies, sugar, celery seeds and mustard seeds in large saucepan. Bring slowly to boil and simmer 3 minutes, stirring until sugar dissolves. Add vegetables and simmer for 12 minutes.

3   Remove from heat. Pack vegetables into warm, sterilised jars. Return pickling mixture to heat and bring to the boil. Pour boiling liquid over vegetables and seal. When cool, label and date.

Beetroot and Cabbage Relish

Cooked fresh beetroot may replace canned beetroot if available. Beetroot and Cabbage Relish teams beautifully with roast pork and crackling.

PREPARATION TIME: *15 minutes*
COOKING TIME: *5 minutes*
MAKES *5 cups*

450 g can sliced beetroot
3 cups finely shredded cabbage
1 onion, thinly sliced
¾ cup red wine vinegar
¾ cup sugar
1 teaspoon salt

1   Drain beetroot and cut into thin strips; reserve juice. Combine beetroot, cabbage and onion in large bowl.

2   Combine reserved juice, vinegar, sugar and salt in large saucepan or boiler. Stir over heat until sugar dissolves. Bring to the boil and remove from heat.

3   Pack beetroot and cabbage mixture into warm, sterilised jars. Pour hot vinegar mixture over vegetables and seal. When cool, label and date.

4   Store 2 days in refrigerator before opening to allow flavours to mellow.

Vegetable Pickles and Beetroot and Cabbage Relish

When pickling onions, blanch whole onions in boiling water for 1 minute. The skins simply slip off.

Pickled Oranges

Pickled oranges can be set with gelatine as a refreshing summer fruit mould or may be added to fruit punch of your choice.

PREPARATION TIME: *20 minutes*
COOKING TIME: *20 minutes*
MAKES *2 litres*

4 medium oranges
¼ teaspoon bicarbonate of soda
2 cups white wine vinegar
1½ cups sugar
1 cup honey
1 teaspoon whole allspice
12 whole cloves
1 cinnamon stick
250 g seedless white grapes

1   Halve oranges and cut each half into four. Put orange wedges and soda into a large saucepan or boiler and cover with water. Bring slowly to boil and boil steadily, uncovered, 7 minutes; drain.

2   Place remaining ingredients except grapes in a large saucepan or boiler. Bring slowly to boil, stirring until sugar is dissolved. Add oranges to saucepan, simmer uncovered for 15 minutes and then add grapes to saucepan.

3   Remove from heat. Pack fruit into warm sterilised jars and add whole allspice and cinnamon. Return pickling mixture to heat and bring to boil. Pour boiling liquid over fruit and seal.

4   When cool, label and date. Store 10 days before opening to mellow flavours.

Pickled Lemons

Use slightly under-ripe lemons for this recipe. (Limes may replace lemons.) Serve with curries or cold roast meats.

PREPARATION TIME: *20 minutes plus overnight soaking*
COOKING TIME: *1 hour*
MAKES *2 litres*

2 kg lemons
½ cup salt
1.5 litres water
1 tablespoon turmeric
1 tablespoon curry powder
½ teaspoon chilli powder
½ teaspoon cayenne pepper
¼ teaspoon ground cloves
1 teaspoon garam masala
½ cup plain flour
2 cups malt vinegar
4 cloves garlic, crushed
1½ cups sugar
¼ cup finely chopped fresh ginger

1   Cut lemons lengthwise into four, then each quarter into 4 pieces. Mix salt and water together, pour over lemons and allow to stand overnight.

2   Next day, cook gently for about 30 minutes or until the lemon rind feels tender. Strain and discard liquid. Mix together the turmeric, curry powder, chilli powder, cayenne pepper, ground cloves, garam masala and the flour. Stir in vinegar to make a smooth paste.

3   Add garlic, sugar and fresh ginger to the lemons. Stir in the remaining vinegar and heat gently, stirring until sugar has dissolved and mixture is boiling. Stir a little of the hot liquid into the curry paste and then back into the saucepan. Continue cooking, stirring constantly for 5 minutes.

4   Spoon into warm, sterilised jars and seal. Label and date when cool.

Citrus fruits, which include the orange, lemon, lime, grapefruit, tangerine and cumquat, comprise one of the largest groups of fruits found in tropical and subtropical regions. When buying any citrus fruit look for firm, heavy and well shaped fruit. As a rule smooth, thin-skinned fruits yield the most juice.

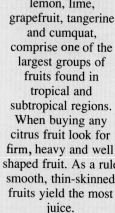

Pickled Oranges and Pickled Lemons

WINTER CHUTNEYS

Lemon Chutney
81

Beetroot Orange Chutney
81

Eggplant Relish
81

Pear Chutney
82

Apple Chutney
82

Orange Apricot Chutney
82

Lemon Chutney

Combine ½ cup Lemon Chutney with ¼ cup chopped mint. Serve with your favourite curry.

PREPARATION TIME: *15 minutes plus overnight soaking*
COOKING TIME: *45 minutes*
MAKES *1 litre*

5 large lemons, chopped and seeds removed
2 large brown onions, chopped
2 teaspoons salt
2 large green cooking apples, peeled and chopped
2 cups malt vinegar
2 cups brown sugar
10 cardamom pods, split (retain seeds)
1 cup chopped dates

1   Place chopped lemons and onions in a glass bowl and sprinkle with salt. Allow to stand overnight then pour out liquid.

2   Place lemons, onions and all remaining ingredients in a large saucepan or boiler and stir well. Bring to the boil, stirring occasionally.

3   Cook until lemon is tender and mixture is thick, about 35–40 minutes. Remove from heat and spoon into warm, sterilised jars and seal. When cool, label and date.

Beetroot Orange Chutney

Use fresh beetroot cooked until just tender for this recipe. Place heaped spoonful of Beetroot Orange Chutney on top of foil baked potatoes and top with spoonful of sour cream. Garnish with grated orange rind. Serve as an entrée or for a light luncheon with salad.

PREPARATION TIME: *15 minutes*
COOKING TIME: *1 hour 5 minutes*
MAKES *1 litre*

500 g fresh cooked beetroot
2 large green apples, peeled and cored
2 oranges

1 cup firmly packed brown sugar
1 cup red wine vinegar

1   Cut beetroot and apples into large dice. Keep separate.

2   Peel oranges, removing pith from peel and flesh. Cut peel into thin strips and chop flesh, discarding pips.

3   Place orange peel and flesh in large heavy saucepan or boiler with the apples, sugar and vinegar. Heat, stirring until boiling. Reduce heat and simmer 30 minutes.

4   Add beetroot and simmer 15 minutes more. Transfer to warm, sterilised jars and cover at once with airtight lids. When cool, label and date. Enjoy at once, or store up to 6 months.

Eggplant Relish

Fold 1 cup of yoghurt and 2 tablespoons finely chopped parsley into Eggplant Relish. Serve with curries, as a dip or as a filling for Lebanese bread.

PREPARATION TIME: *15 minutes*
COOKING TIME: *15 minutes*
MAKES *3 cups*

1 large eggplant
3 tablespoons oil
2 cloves garlic, crushed
1 green capsicum, chopped (Green pepper)
1 onion, chopped
¼ cup chopped fresh basil

1   Cut eggplant into 1 cm cubes. Heat oil in large saucepan.

2   Add eggplant, garlic, capsicum and onion to pan. Stir over heat until onion is soft.

3   Remove from heat and stir in basil; cool. Spoon mixture into airtight container, label and date. Store in refrigerator until required.

Canned fruit can be used in chutneys when fresh is out of season.

Pear Chutney

Any variety of pear can be used for this chutney. Add 2 tablespoons of Pear Chutney to meatloaf mixture, or serve as an accompaniment to pork.

PREPARATION TIME: *1 hour*
COOKING TIME: *1 hour*
MAKES *about 1 litre*

1.25 kg pears
1 large green apple
2 large onions, diced
1 tablespoon grated lemon rind
1 tablespoon grated orange rind
¾ cup raisins
1 cup sugar
1¼ cups white vinegar
1 cup water
½ teaspoon ground ginger
¼ teaspoon ground cloves
1 teaspoon salt

1   Peel and core pears and apples and chop into small pieces.

2   Combine all ingredients in large saucepan or boiler. Bring to the boil, stirring until sugar has dissolved. Simmer 1 hour, stirring occasionally.

3   Pour mixture into warm, sterilised jars and seal. When cool, label and date.

Store dried fruits in an airtight container, add a strip of orange rind to the container to preserve quality; renew this when necessary. Store container in a cool dark cupboard.

Apple Chutney

Spread Apple Chutney onto slices of leg ham, roll up tightly and serve on an antipasto platter.

PREPARATION TIME: *30 minutes*
COOKING TIME: *1 hour 20 minutes*
MAKES *2 litres*

1.5 kg green apples
2 onions
1 red capsicum
1 stick celery
2 cloves garlic, crushed
1.25 litres white vinegar
¾ cup raisins
1 cup sugar
1 tablespoon dry mustard powder
1 tablespoon salt
1 tablespoon chopped fresh basil

1   Peel apples and onions. Finely chop apples, onions, capsicum, celery and raisins.

2   Place apples, onions, capsicum, celery, garlic and vinegar in a large saucepan. Bring slowly to the boil and simmer, uncovered, for 30 minutes, stirring occasionally. Add to saucepan remaining ingredients, bring slowly to the boil and simmer for about 45 minutes until mixture is thick, stirring occasionally.

3   Remove cooked chutney from the heat and stand 5 minutes. Spoon into warm, sterilised jars and seal immediately. When cool, label and date.

Orange Apricot Chutney

Add 2 tablespoons Orange Apricot Chutney to pan after searing pork steaks. Add a little orange juice or water to thin out.

PREPARATION TIME: *20 minutes*
plus 1 hour standing
COOKING TIME: *1 hour*
MAKES *2 litres*

500 g dried apricots
4 medium oranges
2 onions, diced
1 cup sultanas
100 g glacé pineapple
2 cloves garlic, crushed
1 tablespoon salt
1 tablespoon whole allspice
1 tablespoon yellow mustard seeds
6 whole cloves
3 cups brown sugar
2½ cups cider vinegar

1   Halve apricots and soak in boiling water for 1 hour. Peel oranges, shred rind thinly and chop flesh coarsely.

2   Drain apricots. Place all ingredients in a large saucepan or boiler. Bring slowly to the boil, and simmer for 1 hour or until mixture is thick, stirring constantly.

3   Remove chutney from the heat and stand 5 minutes. Pour into warm, sterilised jars and seal immediately. When cool, label and date.

Orange Apricot Chutney, Pear Chutney, Apple Chutney served with brandy flamed rack of veal

PICKLES

Pickles, unlike chutneys, retain the shape and texture of the fruit or vegetables on pickling. The pickling liquid can be a mixture of sugar and vinegar, a salt mixture (brine), spiced vinegar or a thickened mustard and vinegar mixture.

The produce to be pickled can be either raw or cooked, depending on the recipe. However, raw fruits or vegetables must always be salted first to reduce the water content of the vegetable, making the pickling process more effective.

STAGES IN PREPARATION

Preparation of Fruits and Vegetables Cut away any bruised or damaged area and cut the produce as desired. If a clear pickling liquid is to be used, produce looks best if cut into identical shapes and sizes. Vegetables and fruits used for pickles are cut larger than those used for making chutneys.

The Second Stage This will vary depending on the pickling method being used. It may be cooking the produce in a vinegar mixture, or it may be soaking the produce in salt or a brine mixture to remove excess moisture — in which case the salt must be rinsed off and drained prior to packing into jars.

1 *Cut fruit or vegetables as desired, removing any bruised or damaged pieces.*

2 *Place fruit in a glass bowl and sprinkle each layer with salt. Cover and stand for 3 days.*

3 *Using a colander to drain fruit, rinse fruit with cold water and drain well.*

4 *Place fruit, vinegar and spices in a large saucepan. Stir until hot, add sugar, and stir until dissolved.*

Bottling The produce is packed into warm, sterilised jars before the pickling mixture is poured over. The produce should be packed to the top of the jar. After pouring over the pickling mixture the air bubbles should be removed by gently tapping the jar on the bench top which will cause air bubbles to rise to the surface. Ensure the liquid covers the produce. Seal with a lid which the vinegar will not corrode. Suitable lids include plastic coated metal, cork and greaseproof paper or cork topped with a wax covering.

Storing Store pickles for at least 1 month before eating to enjoy the full flavours. Pickles store well for a long time — however check regularly to ensure the pickling mixture is not evaporating through a poor seal. If this does happen, use the pickles immediately or if they have dried, discard them.

6 Pour pickling liquid over fruit, making sure liquid covers all the fruit. Tap jar lightly on bench to remove air.

5 Use tongs to pack fruit in warm sterilised jars. Pack fruit to the top of the jar.

CHUTNEYS

Chutneys are produced by cooking together fruit and vegetables, and both sugar *and* vinegar, with the addition of spices and flavourings, until thick and pulpy.

Chutneys store well if kept in a cool place, provided they have been sealed properly. The choice of vinegar is extremely important. Unless a vinegar with a high acid content is used, the chutney will have a poor keeping quality. Good quality vinegars not only have a high acid content but have a flavour superior to lesser quality vinegars.

Chutneys often contain brown sugar in contrast to most other preserves, which use white. This gives the chutney its characteristic flavour and colour.

The combinations of fruits and vegetables to make chutney are endless, but often dried fruits are added, producing an interesting full-flavoured chutney. Chutneys are simple to make and require minimal attention during cooking.

STAGES IN MAKING

1 Peel, core and chop fruits into small pieces. Wash, trim and cut vegetables into small pieces.

2 Place fruits, vegetables, vinegar and spices in a large saucepan. Stir in sugar.

3 Simmer mixture over low heat, stirring occasionally until mixture is thick and pulpy.

Fruit and Vegetable Preparation Fruits and vegetables should be cut into fairly small pieces. It is possible when making chutneys to use bruised and damaged produce, provided the affected area is cut away prior to using.

Cooking the Chutney All the ingredients are placed in a large heavy based pan and stirred over the heat until the sugar dissolves. The mixture continues to cook over a medium heat until thick and pulpy and leaving the side of the pan. It is essential the mixture is stirred regularly particularly towards the end of cooking to prevent scorching to the base of the mixture.

Bottling The mixture is spooned into warm, sterilised bottles. If any air bubbles are visible, tap the jar gently on the bench top and insert a skewer into the mixture to release the air. Ensure lids are not metal, which the vinegar will corrode in a very short time.

Storing Chutneys are best stored for at least 1 month prior to using to allow time for the flavours to develop and mellow.

4 Spoon chutney into warm sterilised jars. Insert a skewer into mixture to remove air bubbles.

5 Seal warm bottled chutney with a non-corrosive lid — a plastic lid is ideal.

6 When cool, label and date chutney. Store in a cool dark cupboard for 6–8 weeks.

Spring

Spring's celebration of seasonal berries has a fragrance and sweetness not found in other fruits. To enjoy these luscious fruits year round, preserve them. Try our Strawberry Liqueur Jam or Strawberry Conserve. Spring is also the time to delight in lush tropical fruits like mango and pawpaw which combine beautifully to produce vividly coloured jams and jellies. Preserve the early season's vegetables: enjoy Italian Mustard Fruits, spicy Green Tomato Chutney and flavorsome Apple Rhubarb and Mint Chutney.

Strawberry Liqueur Jam served with cream choux puffs

SPRING JAMS

Strawberry and Apple Jam
91

Fruit Salad Jam
91

Strawberry Liqueur Jam
91

Pawpaw Jam
92

Strawberry Conserve
92

Mint Jelly
92

Carrot and Rhubarb Preserve
93

Green Tomato Jam
93

Strawberry and Apple Jam

Spread peeled sliced pears with Strawberry and Apple Jam, cover with crumble topping and bake.

PREPARATION TIME: *15 minutes*
COOKING TIME: *1 hour*
MAKES *1.25 litres*

2 x 250 g punnets strawberries
3 large green apples
¼ cup lemon juice
2 cups water
1 kg sugar, warmed

1 Wash, hull and halve the strawberries. Peel, core and quarter the apples, then cut the quarters into thin slices.

2 Put fruit, lemon juice and water into a large heavy based saucepan or boiler. Bring to boiling point and simmer with lid on until fruit is tender. Remove lid.

3 Add the warmed sugar and stir until sugar dissolves. Increase heat, stirring frequently and cook until setting point is reached.

4 Remove from heat and stand 5 minutes. Pour into warm sterilised jars and seal. When cool, label and date.

Fruit Salad Jam

Spoon 1 teaspoon of Fruit Salad Jam into tartlet cases and top with sweetened cream. Decorate with fresh passionfruit pulp and banana slices dipped in lemon.

PREPARATION TIME: *45 minutes plus overnight standing*
COOKING TIME: *1½ hours*
MAKES *2 litres*

1 medium lemon
4 medium oranges
1.25 litres water
1 kg pineapple
4 passionfruit
2 bananas
1.5 kg sugar, warmed

1 Cut the lemon and oranges into thin slices. Put into a container, add the water and leave overnight. Next day peel the pineapple, remove the core and eyes and finely chop. Pulp the passionfruit and slice the bananas.

2 Put lemon and orange slices with soaking water into a heavy based saucepan or boiler. Bring to simmer and cook until rinds are tender. Add chopped pineapple, sliced bananas and passionfruit pulp. Cook 5 minutes at simmering point.

3 Add the warmed sugar and stir until sugar dissolves; then boil steadily, stirring frequently until jam reaches setting point.

4 Remove from heat and stand 5 minutes. Turn into warm, sterilised jars. When cool, label and date.

Strawberry Liqueur Jam

This delightful jam is a breeze to make using our microwave method. Sandwich together fresh choux puffs with Strawberry Liqueur Jam and whipped cream. Serve with coffee and liqueur.

PREPARATION TIME: *15 minutes*
COOKING TIME: *35 plus 4 minutes (650 watt Microwave)*
MAKES *500 mL*

500 g strawberries
1 medium green apple
juice 1 lime
1¾ cups sugar
2 tablespoons Grand Marnier or other orange liqueur

1 Wash and hull strawberries. Peel, core and finely chop apple. Add lime juice and stand covered 30 minutes.

2 Microwave the fruit and juice for 4 minutes on High.

3 Add sugar and stir through; microwave 35 minutes on High, stirring every 10 minutes.

4 Stand 5 minutes, pour into warm, sterilised glasses and seal. When cool, label and date.

Pikelets (drop scones or small pancakes) are enjoyed warm or cold with butter or cream and sweet full-flavoured jam.

Scones are always firm favourites, and they can be mixed and baked within 30 minutes. Before baking, brush scones with buttermilk for golden shiny tops. Melted butter helps brown the tops but gives less shine. After baking, scones may be cooled on a cake rack for crisp scones or wrapped in a clean tea towel for softer scones.

Pawpaw Jam

Accompany chilled peach halves with warm Pawpaw Jam. Top peach halves with extra toasted almonds and a fresh mint leaf. Serve with ice-cream for a luscious dessert.

PREPARATION TIME: *20 minutes*
COOKING TIME: *35 minutes*
MAKES *1 litre*

1.5 kg pawpaw (not too ripe)
1 x 200 g pkt preserved ginger
½ cup lemon juice
2 cups sugar, warmed

1   Peel and seed pawpaw; chop flesh coarsely. Finely chop ginger.

2   Put pawpaw, ginger and lemon juice into a large heavy saucepan or boiler. Cover and bring to the boil. Simmer with lid on until pawpaw is tender, about 7–10 minutes. Remove the lid.

3   Add the warmed sugar and stir over a low heat until sugar has dissolved. Bring to boil again and boil rapidly stirring frequently until jam reaches setting point, about 25 minutes.

4   Remove from heat and stand 1–2 minutes. Pour into warm, sterilised jars and seal immediately. When cool, label and date.

Strawberry Conserve

Use strawberries that are just ripe for this traditional Strawberry Conserve. Make small quantities only. Serve with scones or pikelets or place 1 teaspoon of Strawberry Conserve in the base of individual vanilla soufflés before baking.

PREPARATION TIME: *15 minutes plus overnight soaking*
COOKING TIME: *35 minutes*
MAKES *1½ cups*

500 g strawberries
1½ cups sugar

1   Wash and drain fruit then remove stalks. Cover fruit with ½ cup of sugar and stand overnight.

2   Strain liquid from strawberries. Place in saucepan, add remaining sugar and stir over low heat for 10 minutes. Do not allow to boil.

3   Add fruit, cooking till setting point is reached, about 20–30 minutes.

4   Ladle into warm, sterilised jars. When cool, seal and label.

Mint Jelly

This is a traditional accompaniment to roast lamb.

PREPARATION TIME: *30 minutes*
COOKING TIME: *45 minutes*
MAKES *3½ cups*

1 kg green apples
1 litre water
½ cup lemon juice
2 cups fresh mint leaves
sugar
green colouring, optional

1   Cut apples into thick slices but do not peel or core.

2   Combine apples, water, lemon juice and mint leaves in large saucepan or boiler. Bring to the boil and boil slowly, uncovered, for about 10 minutes. Break up apples with a wooden spoon and boil slowly for a further 15 minutes or until apples are soft and pulpy.

3   Strain mixture through muslin suspended over a bowl and stand overnight. Measure strained juice and return to saucepan. Add 1 cup of warmed sugar for each cup of juice and stir over heat until sugar is dissolved. Bring to the boil and boil rapidly until setting point is reached. Add a few drops of colouring to mixture to give desired colour.

4   Remove mixture from heat and stand 2 minutes. Pour into warm, sterilised jars. Seal when cold. Label and date.

Warming the sugar prior to adding to jams and jellies will help prevent scum from forming on the surface.

Carrot and Rhubarb Preserve

Use Carrot and Rhubarb Preserve as a filling for sponge cakes and fruit tartlets.

PREPARATION TIME: *30 minutes*
COOKING TIME: *45 minutes*
MAKES *8 cups*

1 kg carrots, peeled and thinly sliced
1 kg rhubarb, thinly sliced
1 kg sugar, warmed

1   Place carrots in saucepan with enough water to cover. Bring to the boil, covered, until carrots are tender. Drain carrots and reserve ½ cup cooking liquid.

2   Purée carrots and reserved liquid in food processor until smooth. Transfer to large saucepan or boiler.

3   Add rhubarb and the warmed sugar to saucepan and stir until sugar is dissolved. Boil slowly, uncovered for about 20 minutes or until thickened.

4   Remove mixture from heat and pour into warm, sterilised jars. Seal when cold. Label and date.

Green Tomato Jam

Green Tomato Jam is a tasty topping for hot scones and teacakes; serve with lashings of butter.

PREPARATION TIME: *15 minutes*
COOKING TIME: *1 hour*
MAKES *3 cups*

1 kg green tomatoes
1 lemon
1 cup water
3 cups sugar

1   Slice the tomatoes and lemon thinly.

2   Put the tomatoes, lemon, sugar and water into a saucepan and bring to the boil, stirring until sugar has dissolved. Reduce heat and simmer for 1 hour, or until tomatoes are transparent and setting point has been reached.

3   Ladle into warm, sterilised jars and seal airtight. Label and date when cool.

Strawberry Conserve and Pawpaw Jam

Put a use-by date on the label of preserves.

93

SPRING PICKLES

Spiced Pawpaw
95

Processor Vegetable Relish
95

Italian Mustard Fruits
96

Zucchini Pickle
96

Pickled Onions
96

Continental Pickles
98

Chunky Piccalilli
98

Italian Style Pickles
99

Spiced Pawpaw

Serve Spiced Pawpaw with smoked turkey, chicken, fish or seafood.

PREPARATION TIME: *15 minutes*
plus overnight standing
COOKING TIME: *40 minutes*
MAKES *1 litre*

1 large ripe firm pawpaw
sugar
white vinegar
1 tablespoon whole cloves
2 teaspoons whole allspice
1 x 5 cm piece cinnamon stick

1   Peel pawpaw, cut into halves and scrape out the seeds. Cut each half into finger length pieces. Weigh them and allow 1½ cups sugar for each 50 g fruit. Put fruit into a container, sprinkle the sugar over and leave overnight.

2   Put fruit and syrup into a large saucepan or boiler and heat gently, stirring until sugar has dissolved; then simmer until pawpaw looks transparent. Do not overcook. Drain syrup from fruit, measure and allow ¾ cup vinegar for 2½ cups syrup. Add the vinegar to the syrup with cloves, allspice and lightly crushed cinnamon stick.

3   Bring to boiling point, cover and boil gently for 10 minutes. Put aside until cold and then strain. Replace syrup in pan, add pawpaw and cook 7 minutes.

4   Remove from heat, lift pawpaw slices out with a slotted spoon and put into sterilised jars. Bring syrup back to boil and spoon over pawpaw. Cool before sealing. Label and date.

Processor Vegetable Relish

This quick and easy Vegetable Relish makes a tasty sandwich filling.

PREPARATION TIME: *45 minutes*
plus overnight standing
COOKING TIME: *10 minutes*
MAKES *3.5 litres*

1.5 kg ripe tomatoes
2 medium onions
1 kg zucchini
500 g red capsicums
500 g green capsicums
2 cloves garlic
2 tablespoons salt
2 cups cider vinegar
2 cups sugar
1 cup water
½ cup cornflour
2 teaspoons dried thyme leaves
½ teaspoon pepper

1   Peel and coarsely chop tomatoes and onions. Coarsely chop zucchini and capsicums. Combine chopped vegetables in bowl. Process mixture in food processor in several batches until finely chopped. Place mixture in large bowl and sprinkle with salt. Cover and stand overnight.

2   Next day, place vegetable mixture in colander and drain away excess liquid. Place vegetable mixture in large saucepan or boiler, add vinegar and sugar and stir over heat until sugar is dissolved. Bring to the boil and simmer for 5 minutes.

3   Combine water, cornflour, thyme and pepper in small bowl; blend until smooth. Add to pan and bring to the boil, stirring constantly. Simmer until thickened. Remove from heat. Pour mixture into warm, sterilised jars. Seal. When cool, label and date.

For a full-flavoured pickle prepare spiced vinegar well in advance. Flavour vinegar with peppercorns, mustard seeds and cloves.

Spiced Pawpaw

Italian Mustard Fruits

Any fresh seasonal fruits may be used for this recipe. Serve as part of an antipasto, with roast chicken or smoked turkey.

PREPARATION TIME: *35 minutes*
COOKING TIME: *10 minutes*
MAKES *2 litres*

1 kg fresh fruits in season
500 g assorted glacé fruit
2½ cups sugar
½ cup red wine vinegar
⅓ cup lemon juice
⅓ cup water
3 tablespoons Dijon mustard
1 teaspoon yellow mustard seeds
2 cloves garlic, thickly sliced

1   Peel, core and very thickly slice the fresh fruit. Leave glacé fruits whole or cut into chunks. Combine all fruits in a bowl.

2   In a large heavy saucepan or boiler combine sugar, vinegar, lemon juice and water. Heat until boiling, stirring to dissolve sugar. Boil 5 minutes. Stir in mustard, seeds, garlic and prepared fruits. Simmer gently for about 5 minutes.

3   Ladle fruit and syrup into warm, sterilised jars and seal. When cool, label and date. Refrigerate at least 1 week while flavours mellow.

Zucchini Pickle

Choose small to medium zucchini for this pickle. Serve as a side dish for steaks, chops, chicken and seafood.

PREPARATION TIME: *30 minutes*
plus 2 hours standing
COOKING TIME: *5 minutes*
MAKES *1.5 litres*

1 kg zucchini
2 medium onions
¼ cup salt
2¼ cups white vinegar
1 cup sugar
2 teaspoons mustard seeds
1 teaspoon turmeric
½ teaspoon dry mustard

1   Wash zucchini, trim ends and slice very thinly. Quarter the onions lengthwise and separate into layers. Combine zucchini, onions and salt with enough water to cover in large bowl; stir well. Stand 1 hour then drain.

2   Combine remaining ingredients in large saucepan or boiler. Bring to the boil, stirring until sugar is dissolved. Pour hot vinegar mixture over zucchini mixture and stand 1 hour.

3   Transfer zucchini and vinegar mixture to the large saucepan. Bring to the boil and simmer for 3 minutes.

4   Spoon into warm, sterilised jars ensuring zucchini is covered with cooking liquid. Seal. When cold, label and date.

Pickled Onions

Serve onions with salads or cheese.

PREPARATION TIME: *1 hour plus 2 days*
standing
COOKING TIME: *10 minutes*
MAKES *about 1.5 litres*

1 kg pickling onions
1 cup salt
2 litres water
625mL vinegar
½ cup sugar
6 black peppercorns
6 whole cloves
2.5 cm piece cinnamon stick
4 blades mace
2 teaspoons whole allspice
red chillies

1   Peel onions and place in large bowl with salt and water; stir well. Cover and stand 2 days, stirring occasionally.

2   Combine remaining ingredients, except chillies, in large saucepan or boiler. Bring slowly to the boil. Remove from heat and stand 1 hour then strain.

3   Pack drained onions into warm, sterilised jars. Place a few chillies in each jar.

4   Pour spiced vinegar over onions and seal. When cool, label and date.

The word vinegar comes from the French *vinaigre*, literally 'sour wine'. Types of vinegar include red or white wine vinegar made from grape fermentation, cider vinegar from apples, and malt vinegar from barley.

Pickled Onions served as part of a ploughman's lunch

Pickling spices are blends of spices that include black pepper, yellow mustard seeds, cloves, coriander seeds, mace, cinnamon sticks and allspice.

Fruits high in acid content — apples, bilberries, blackcurrants, cherries (morello or under-ripe), citrus fruits, cranberries, damsons, gooseberries, greengages, loganberries, pineapples, plums (under-ripe), redcurrants.

Continental Pickles

White savoy or Chinese cabbage is best for this recipe. Serve ½ cup drained Continental Pickles on crisp baked pita bread wedges with a dollop of sour cream, as an entrée.

PREPARATION TIME: *20 minutes*
COOKING TIME: *20 minutes*
MAKES *2 litres*

½ small cabbage
2 onions
1 red capsicum
1 green capsicum
3 cucumbers
2 cups white vinegar
1 cup water
½ cup honey
2 sprigs fresh oregano
1 teaspoon black peppercorns
1 tablespoon seeded mustard

1   Finely shred cabbage. Slice onions, capsicum and cucumbers thinly.

2   Place vinegar, water, honey, oregano, peppercorns and mustard in a large saucepan or boiler. Bring slowly to boil and simmer 2 minutes. Add to saucepan all vegetables, except cabbage, and simmer 10 minutes. Stir in cabbage and simmer a further 5 minutes, stirring occasionally.

3   Remove from heat. Pack vegetables into warm, sterilised jars. Return pickling mixture to heat and bring to the boil. Pour boiling liquid over vegetables and seal. When cool, label and date.

Chunky Piccalilli

Add 500 mL jar of Chunky Piccalilly to 500 g of cubed and seared casserole meat. Cover with water and simmer gently until meat is tender. Season with pepper.

PREPARATION TIME: *25 minutes*
plus overnight standing
COOKING TIME: *20 minutes*
MAKES *2 litres*

1 small cauliflower
2 sticks celery
1 carrot
2 zucchini
1 small eggplant
2 tablespoons salt
2 tablespoons plain flour
1¾ cups cider vinegar
½ cup sugar
2 tablespoons yellow mustard seeds
1 tablespoon turmeric
1 tablespoon mustard powder
2 teaspoons Mexican chilli powder

1   Wash and break cauliflower into small pieces. Coarsely chop celery, carrot, zucchini and eggplant. Place vegetables in a large bowl, sprinkle with salt, cover with plastic wrap and stand overnight. Rinse vegetables and drain.

2   Blend flour with ¼ cup vinegar, set aside. Place remaining vinegar, sugar, mustard seeds, turmeric, mustard powder and chilli powder in a large saucepan or boiler. Bring slowly to the boil and simmer for 3 minutes, stirring until sugar is dissolved.

3   Add vegetables to pan, bring slowly to the boil and simmer 12 minutes. Add flour mixture to pan, bring to the boil and simmer a further 5 minutes or until mixture is thick.

4   Remove from heat. Pack vegetables into warm, sterilised jars. Return vinegar mixture to heat and bring to the boil. Pour boiling liquid over vegetables and seal. When cool, label and date. Store 10 days before opening to mellow flavours.

Italian Style Pickles

Serve Italian Style Pickles as a salad with Italian rissoles and fresh crusty bread.

PREPARATION TIME: *30 minutes*
COOKING TIME: *10 minutes*
MAKES *1.5 litres*

1 eggplant
2 teaspoons salt
1 green capsicum
200 g green beans
2 onions
2 cups white vinegar
½ cup sugar
2 cloves garlic, sliced
2 tablespoons fresh oregano leaves
1 cup olive oil
1 cup black olives, drained
1 punnet cherry tomatoes

1   Wash and finely chop eggplant, place in small bowl, sprinkle liberally with salt and stand 30 minutes. Rinse under cold water; drain. Coarsely chop capsicum, beans and peeled onions.

2   Place all ingredients, except the olives and tomatoes, in a large saucepan or boiler. Bring slowly to the boil and simmer uncovered for about 8 minutes, stirring until sugar is dissolved. Stir in olives and tomatoes.

3   Remove from heat. Pack vegetables into warm, sterilised jars. Return liquid to heat and bring to the boil. Pour into warm, sterilised jars and seal. When cool, label and date. Store 7 days before opening to mellow flavours.

Italian Style Pickles

SPRING CHUTNEYS

Golden Chutney
101

Green Tomato Chutney
101

Tomato and Pineapple Relish
101

Rhubarb Chutney
102

Mango and Kiwi Fruit Chutney
102

Green Bean Relish
102

Tropical Coconut Chutney
104

Curried Parsnip Chutney
104

Spicy Green Tomato Chutney
104

Apple, Rhubarb and Mint Chutney
105

Golden Chutney

Serve our Spicy Golden Chutney with ham, chicken, pork and veal.

PREPARATION TIME: *15 minutes*
COOKING TIME: *1 hour*
MAKES *1 litre*

½ large pawpaw (papaya)
½ large rockmelon
1 large pear
1 large onion
⅓ cup sultanas
1 cup sugar
½ cup white vinegar
1 teaspoon sugar
juice 1 orange
1 teaspoon mustard seeds
½ teaspoon ground ginger
½ teaspoon chilli powder

1   Peel the pawpaw and rockmelon and remove seeds. Chop finely. Peel, core and chop pear finely. Finely chop onion.

2   Put all the ingredients into a large saucepan or boiler, bring to boiling point stirring until sugar has dissolved. Then reduce heat and simmer about 50 minutes, stirring frequently.

3   Remove from heat, turn into warm sterilised jars and seal airtight. When cool, label and date.

Green Tomato Chutney

Place teaspoon of Green Tomato Chutney on plain cornchips, sprinkle with grated cheese and bake at 180°C till brown.

PREPARATION TIME: *30 minutes*
COOKING TIME: *45–60 minutes*
MAKES *500 g*

500 g green tomatoes
2 medium onions
1 large green apple, cored
1 green capsicum
3 fresh green chillies
1 clove garlic, crushed

½ cup sugar
1 cup malt vinegar

1   Coarsely chop tomatoes, onions and apples. Dice capsicum, discarding core, seeds and white pith. Slit open chillies, discard seeds and finely chop flesh.

2   Place all ingredients in a heavy based saucepan or boiler. Heat until boiling, stirring until sugar dissolves.

3   Reduce heat and simmer, stirring occasionally until thickened to desired consistency, about 45–60 minutes.

4   Transfer to warm, sterilised jars and seal. When cool, label and date. Mature 2 weeks before opening. Store for up to 6 months.

Tomato and Pineapple Relish

Serve Tomato and Pineapple Relish with pâté or terrine and melba toast or fresh rolls for a light luncheon or supper.

PREPARATION TIME: *1 hour*
COOKING TIME: *1½–2 hours*
MAKES *1.5 litres*

1 kg ripe tomatoes, peeled
2 large green apples
2 medium onions
1 cup finely chopped fresh pineapple
3 cups sugar
¾ cup sultanas
1 tablespoon salt
1 tablespoon whole cloves
1.25 litres malt vinegar

1   Chop the tomatoes coarsely. Peel the apple and onions and chop finely.

2   Put tomatoes, apples, onions, pineapple, sugar, sultanas, salt and cloves into a large saucepan or boiler and stir in half the vinegar. Cook gently, stirring for 5 minutes. Add the remaining vinegar and stir over low heat until sugar has dissolved. Simmer for about 1½ hours or until thick, stirring occasionally.

3   Ladle into warm, sterilised jars and seal. When cool, label and date.

Never seal preserves warm. Seal either while hot or allow to cool completely prior to sealing.

For a quick delicious lunch, sandwich together rye bread, sliced meat such as ham or turkey, and your favourite fruit chutney.

Rhubarb Chutney

Combine 1 cup Rhubarb Chutney with 500 g pork and veal mince. Use as a filling for pastry such as samosas.

PREPARATION TIME: *20 minutes plus overnight standing*
COOKING TIME: *45 minutes*
MAKES *1.5 litres*

250 g dried figs
1 kg rhubarb stalks
1 green capsicum
1 x 200 g pkt dried apples
3 cups dark brown sugar
2 teaspoons chopped fresh ginger
¼ cup soy sauce
5 dried red chillies
1 cup malt vinegar

1   Halve figs and soak in boiling water overnight; drain. Coarsely chop rhubarb and capsicum; finely chop apples.

2   Place all ingredients in a large saucepan or boiler. Bring slowly to boil and simmer for about 45 minutes or until mixture is thick, stirring constantly.

3   Remove cooked chutney from the heat and stand 5 minutes. Pour into warm, sterilised jars and seal immediately. When cool, label and date.

> To prevent tears when chopping onions, place in the freezer for 1 hour prior to using.

Excellent ✶

Mango and Kiwi Fruit Chutney

This chutney makes a delicious accompaniment to ham or chicken.

PREPARATION TIME: *40 minutes*
✶ *plus overnight standing*
COOKING TIME: *1½–2 hours*
MAKES *1.5 litres*

6 large mangoes
8 kiwi fruit
2 small red chillies, seeded and finely chopped
2 tablespoons grated fresh ginger
2 large cloves garlic
3 teaspoons salt
2 cups white vinegar) *Second*
3 cups raw sugar _) Day*

1   Peel, stone and chop mangoes, peel and coarsely chop kiwi fruit. Combine mangoes, kiwi fruit, chillies, ginger and garlic. Sprinkle with salt, cover and allow to stand overnight. Drain.

2   Combine vinegar and sugar in a large saucepan or boiler, bring to the boil and simmer 5 minutes. Add all remaining ingredients. Simmer 1¼–1½ hours or until mango is tender and chutney is a good consistency.

3   Pour into warm, sterilised jars and seal. When cool, label and date. Store in a cool dark place.

Green Bean Relish

Green Bean Relish is tasty as an accompaniment to curries and casseroles and as a condiment for cold meats.

PREPARATION TIME: *1 hour*
COOKING TIME: *15 minutes*
MAKES *3 litres*

1 kg green beans
3 onions
6¼ cups malt vinegar
1½ cups sugar
1 tablespoon salt
½ teaspoon pepper
1 tablespoon plain flour
1 tablespoon dry mustard
1 teaspoon turmeric
¼ cup malt vinegar, extra

1   Top and tail beans and slice diagonally. Peel and thinly slice onions.

2   Combine vinegar, sugar, salt and pepper in large saucepan or boiler. Bring to the boil, stirring until sugar has dissolved. Add the beans and onions. Bring to the boil and simmer, uncovered until beans are just tender.

3   Blend flour, mustard and turmeric with extra vinegar. Add to saucepan and stir over heat until mixture boils. Simmer 5 minutes.

4   Spoon mixture into warm, sterilised jars and seal. When cool, label and date.

Mango and Kiwi Fruit Chutney

Tropical Coconut Chutney

Combine an equal quantity of Tropical Coconut Chutney and thickened sour cream. Gently warm through and serve over chicken or fish fillets.

PREPARATION TIME: *60 minutes*
COOKING TIME: *1½–2 hours*
MAKES *1.5 litres*

1 small lemon
5 large mangoes
1 medium pawpaw
1 large onion
1 green capsicum
1 x 125 g packet crystallised ginger
½ cup raisins
1 clove garlic, crushed
½ cup coconut cream
1 cup desiccated coconut
1 cup malt vinegar
1½ cups brown sugar
2 teaspoons cinnamon
1½ teaspoons salt
8 whole cloves
½ teaspoon ground allspice
½ teaspoon white pepper

1   Cut unpeeled lemon into small pieces, removing pips. Peel, seed and coarsely chop mangoes and pawpaw. Chop onion, capsicum and ginger; finely chop raisins.

2   Place all ingredients in a large saucepan or boiler and bring slowly to the boil, stirring until sugar has dissolved. Cook very gently, stirring occasionally, for 1½–2 hours.

3   Turn into warm, sterilised jars and seal airtight. When cool, label and date.

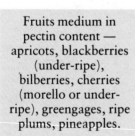

Curried Parsnip Chutney

When buying parsnips, look for a small to medium root. Larger parsnips tend to be woody and tough. Cut out 10 cm rounds of puff pastry. Fill each round with 1 teaspoon Curried Parsnip Chutney and seal edges. Bake until golden.

PREPARATION TIME: *40 minutes*
COOKING TIME: *1 hour 25 minutes*
MAKES *1.5 litres*

1 kg parsnips
3 onions
1 orange
1½ cups vinegar
1 cup water
1½ cups brown sugar
250 g fresh dates
1 tablespoon curry powder
½ teaspoon garam masala
2 teaspoons salt

1   Peel and finely chop parsnips and onions. Peel orange and shred peel thinly; chop flesh coarsely.

2   Place parsnips, onions, orange rind, vinegar and water in a large saucepan or boiler. Bring slowly to boil and simmer uncovered for 1 hour. Add to pan remaining ingredients. Bring slowly to boil and simmer for 25 minutes or until mixture is thick, stirring constantly.

3   Remove cooked chutney from the heat and stand 5 minutes. Pour into warm sterilised jars and seal immediately. When cool, label and date.

Spicy Green Tomato Chutney

Combine ½ cup Spicy Green Tomato Chutney with rice filling for stuffed capsicums. Stir 2 tablespoons into your favourite lamb casserole.

PREPARATION TIME: *30 minutes*
COOKING TIME: *1¾ hours*
MAKES *2.5 litres*

2 kg green tomatoes
4 cooking apples
3 onions
6 dried red chillies
250 g raisins
¼ cup lime juice
2½ cups brown sugar
2¼ cups malt vinegar
2 teaspoons ground cinnamon
1 teaspoon black peppercorns
½ teaspoon caraway seeds

1 Wash and finely chop unpeeled tomatoes and apples. Peel and finely chop onions.

2 Place tomatoes, apples and onions in a large saucepan or boiler. Bring slowly to boil and simmer, uncovered for 45 minutes. Add remaining ingredients to pan. Bring slowly to boil and simmer, uncovered for 1 hour or until mixture is thick, stirring constantly.

3 Remove chutney from the heat and stand 5 minutes. Pour into warm, sterilised jars and seal immediately. When cool, label and date.

Apple, Rhubarb and Mint Chutney

Apple, Rhubarb and Mint Chutney is a delicious accompaniment to roast lamb.

PREPARATION TIME: *20 minutes*
COOKING TIME: *30 minutes*
MAKES *2 cups*

500 g green apples
2 stalks rhubarb
1 onion, chopped
½ cup chopped fresh mint leaves
slivers of peel and juice of 2 lemons
¾ cup sugar
¾ cup cider vinegar
1 teaspoon ground cinnamon

1 Peel, core and chop apples, cut rhubarb into 2.5cm pieces.

2 Place all ingredients in large heavy saucepan or boiler. Heat slowly until boiling, stirring until sugar dissolves. Reduce heat and simmer, stirring occasionally until thickened.

3 Ladle into warm, sterilised jars and cover at once with airtight lids. When cool, label and date.

Microwave Method: Place all ingredients in large bowl. Cover three-quarters of bowl with plastic wrap. Microwave at High power 20–30 minutes. Proceed with step 3 as above.

Clockwise from top left: Apple, Rhubarb and Mint Chutney, Tropical Coconut Chutney, Spicy Green Tomato Chutney, and Curried Parsnip Chutney

Glossary

ALLSPICE: a mildly sharp, fragrant spice, not to be confused with mixed spice. It is sometimes called pimento or Jamaica pepper. Available whole or ground.

BICARBONATE OF SODA: also known as baking soda.

CAPERS: small green buds that are hand-picked, salted and pickled. They add a piquant flavour to foods.

CAPSICUM: sweet peppers, red or green.

CARDAMOM: an aromatic, Asian spice sold as pods or in ground form. Anise or cinnamon can be substituted.

CAYENNE PEPPER: ground red pepper, sweet, pungent and very hot.

CHERRY TOMATOES: small sweet tomatoes also known as Tom Thumb tomatoes.

CHILLI: the dried pods of small capsicums. Use fresh chillies were specified, with great care. As the seeds are the hottest part these can be removed and discarded if preferred.

CINNAMON: a mildly pungent spice, used ground or as sticks (quills).

CLOVES: a sharp, aromatic spice, used whole or ground.

COCONUT, DESICCATED: finely shredded dried coconut.

CORNFLOUR: cornstarch.

DIJON MUSTARD: pale yellow mustard from France.

EGGPLANT: aubergine.

GARAM MASALA: a mixture of ground spices that includes cardamom, clove, cumin and pepper.

GINGER: fresh root ginger available from a greengrocer's or fruiterer's. It is usually peeled and chopped before using. Ground ginger is a strong, pungent spice. Preserved or crystallised ginger is peeled root ginger preserved in sugar syrup.

GLACÉ FRUITS: fruits coated with sugar to give an attractive edible finish.

GOLDEN SYRUP: honey, maple or pancake syrup can be substituted.

HORSERADISH: a root of the mustard family, it has a hot pungent taste. Available as relish or cream.

KIWI FRUIT: Chinese gooseberry.

MACADAMIA NUTS: sweet butter-flavoured nuts, native to Australia.

MACE: the lacy outer covering of nutmeg. Available as a blade or tendril or ground.

MIXED FRUIT: a mixture of raisins, sultanas, currants and cherries, with mixed crystallised citrus peel.

MIXED PEEL: a mixture of crystallised citrus peel.

MIXED SPICE: (not to be confused with allspice) a combination of spices including allspice, nutmeg and cinnamon, used for flavouring.

MUSTARD SEEDS: black, brown, white and yellow seeds from the mustard plant. The dark seeds give aroma while the lighter seeds give pungency.

NUTMEG: a strongly aromatic spice. Use the powdered form or grated whole nutmeg.

ORANGE-FLOWER WATER: an extract of orange flowers and orange rind, available at health food stores.

PASSIONFRUIT: fruit of the passionflower vine, also known as granadilla.

PAWPAW: papaya.

PEPPER: a strongly piquant spice sold ground or as whole peppercorns, available black or white.

PLAIN FLOUR: all-purpose flour.

PUMPKIN: member of the squash family, with sweet orange flesh.

QUINCE: fruit rich in pectin, ideal for jam and jelly making.

RAISINS: dried, dark sweet grapes.

RIND: zest.

ROCKMELON: also known as ogen melon or cantaloupe.

ROSEWATER: extract of rose petals, available from Asian and health food stores.

SOY SAUCE: made from soya beans, it adds richness and flavour. A great variety is available from Asian stores and supermarkets.

SPICES: the most commonly used spices are nutmeg, cinnamon, cloves, ginger, allspice, mixed spice and pepper. Store spices in an airtight container in a dark cupboard for no longer than 6 months.

STAR ANISE: star-shaped fruit which is dried and has a pungent aniseed flavour.

SUGAR: white granulated sugar.

BROWN SUGAR: soft brown sugar with molasses present.

SULTANAS: dried, seedless white grapes.

TREACLE: honey or maple syrup can be substituted.

TURMERIC: dried root sold ground. It has a slightly bitter flavour and brilliant yellow colour. Often used in Indian cooking.

VANILLA BEAN: vanilla pod.

VINEGAR: a by-product of fermentation. Many varieties are available — red or white wine vinegar made from grapes, cider vinegar from apples, malt vinegar from barley. Distilled vinegars are best for preserving owing to their higher acetic acid content.

ZUCCHINI: courgette.

Equipment

CAN, CANNED: tin, tinned.

GREASEPROOF PAPER: waxproof paper.

PLASTIC WRAP: cling film.

PUNNET: small box or basket containing about 250 g fruit.

SEEDED: stoned or pitted — stone removed and discarded.

INDEX

This edition published in 1991 in association with Charles Letts & Co. Limited, London, Edinburgh, New York, Toronto, Sydney; Head Office: Diary House, Borough Road, London SE1 1DW.
First published by **Murdoch Books**, a division of Murdoch Magazines Pty Ltd
213 Miller Street, North Sydney NSW 2060

Murdoch Books Food Editor: Jo Anne Calabria
Art Direction and Design: Elaine Rushbrooke
Photography: Ray Joyce
Photographic Assistant: Lynette Manwaring
Illustrations: Barbara Rodanska
Cover Calligraphy: Margrit Eisermann
Family Circle Cookery Editor: Jennene Plummer
Consultant Food Editor: Deborah Hyam
Home Economists: Jane Ash, Kerrie Carr, Voula Mantzouridis, Denise Munro, Helen Talty
Editor: Ingaret Ward
Finished Art: Ivy Hansen
Index: Michael Wyatt

Publisher: Anne Wilson
Publishing Manager: Mark Newman
Managing Editor: Maureen Colman
Production Co-ordinator: Catie Ziller
Marketing Manager: Mark Smith

British Library Cataloguing-in-Publication Data
Jams, Pickles and Chutneys
Includes index.
ISBN 1-85238-179-5
1. Preserves (Series: Letts Country Cottage Collection)
641.85

Printed by Toppan Printing Co. Ltd, Singapore
Typeset by Savage Type Pty Ltd, Brisbane
© Murdoch Books 1990

USEFUL INFORMATION

Recipes are all thoroughly tested, using standard
metric measuring cups and spoons.
All cup and spoon measurements are level.
We have used eggs with an average weight of 55 g
each in all recipes.

WEIGHTS AND MEASURES

In this book, metric measures
and their imperial equivalents
have been rounded out to the
nearest figure that is easy to use.
Different charts from different
authorities vary slightly; the
following are the measures we
have used consistently
throughout our recipes.

OVEN TEMPERATURE CHART

	C	F	Gas Mark
Very slow	120	250	½
Slow	150	300	1–2
Mod. slow	160	325	3
Moderate	180	350	4
Mod. hot	190	375	5–6
Hot	200	400	6–7
Very hot	230	450	8–9

LENGTHS

Metric	Imperial
5 mm	¼ in
1 cm	½ in
2 cm	¾ in
2.5 cm	1 in
5 cm	2 in
6 cm	2½ in
8 cm	3 in
10 cm	4 in
12 cm	5 in
15 cm	6 in
18 cm	7 in
20 cm	8 in
23 cm	9 in
25 cm	10 in
28 cm	11 in
30 cm	12 in
46 cm	18 in
50 cm	20 in
61 cm	24 in
77 cm	30 in

CUP & SPOON MEASURES

A basic metric cup set consists of
1 cup, ½ cup, ⅓ cup and ¼ cup
sizes.

The basic spoon set comprises
1 tablespoon, 1 teaspoon,
½ teaspoon and ¼ teaspoon.

1 cup	250 mL / 8 fl oz
½ cup	125 mL / 4 fl oz
⅓ cup	80 mL / 2½ fl oz
(4 tablespoons)	
¼ cup	60 mL / 2 fl oz
(3 tablespoons)	
1 tablespoon	20 mL
1 teaspoon	5 mL
½ teaspoon	2.5 mL
¼ teaspoon	1.25 mL

LIQUIDS

Metric	Imperial
30 mL	1 fl oz
60 mL	2 fl oz
90 mL	3 fl oz
100 mL	3½ fl oz
125 mL	4 fl oz (½ cup)
155 mL	5 fl oz
170 mL	5½ fl oz (⅔ cup)
185 mL	6 fl oz
200 mL	6½ fl oz
220 mL	7 fl oz
250 mL	8 fl oz (1 cup)
280 mL	9 fl oz
300 mL	9½ fl oz
315 mL	10 fl oz
350 mL	11 fl oz
375 mL	12 fl oz
410 mL	13 fl oz
440 mL	14 fl oz
470 mL	15 fl oz
500 mL	16 fl oz (2 cups)
600 mL	1 pt (20 fl oz)
750 mL	1 pt 5 fl oz (3 cups)
1 litre	1 pt 12 fl oz (4 cups)
(1000 mL)	
1.5 litres	2 pt 8 fl oz (6 cups)

DRY INGREDIENTS

Metric	Imperial
15 g	½ oz
30 g	1 oz
45 g	1½ oz
60 g	2 oz
75 g	2½ oz
90 g	3 oz
100 g	3½ oz
125 g	4 oz
140 g	4½ oz
155 g	5 oz
170 g	5½ oz
185 g	6 oz
200 g	6½ oz
220 g	7 oz
235 g	7½ oz
250 g	8 oz
265 g	8½ oz
280 g	9 oz
300 g	9½ oz
315 g	10 oz
330 g	10½ oz
350 g	11 oz
360 g	11½ oz
375 g	12 oz
400 g	12 ½ oz
410 g	13 oz
425 g	13½ oz
440 g	14 oz
455 g	14½ oz
470 g	15 oz
485 g	15½ oz
500 g	1 lb (16 oz)
750 g	1 lb 8 oz
1 kg (1000 g)	2 lb
1.5 kg	3 lb
2 kg	4 lb
2.5 kg	5 lb

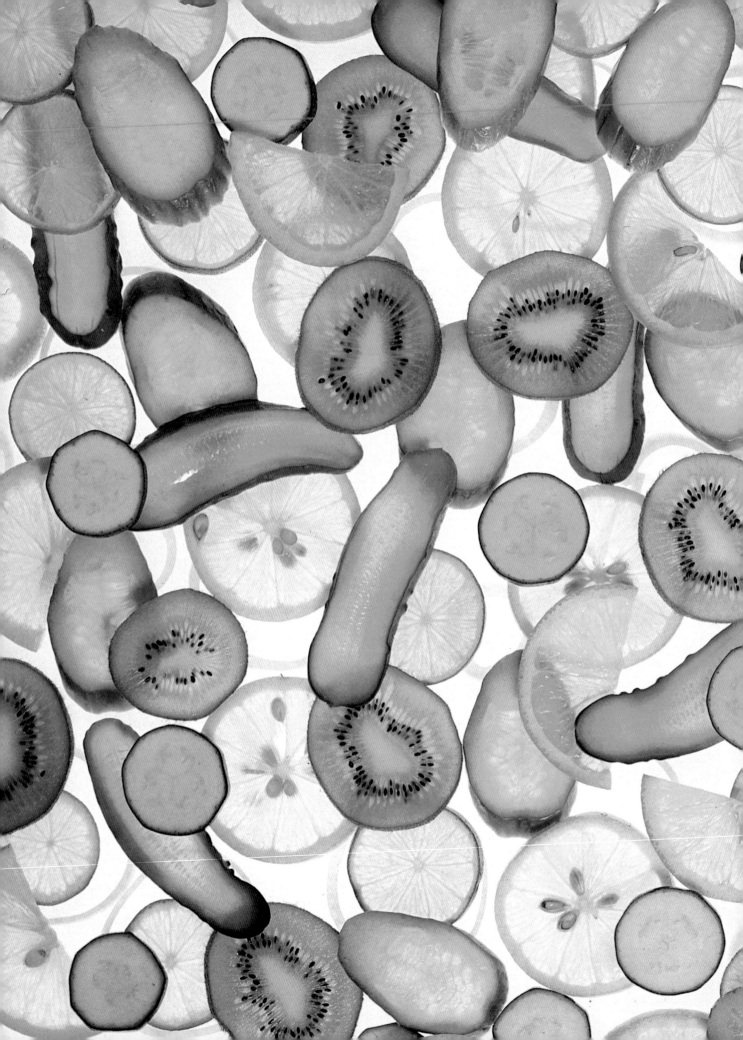